350 Alcohol Ink Papers with Original Origami Patterns

FOLDABLE, DOUBLE-SIDED, EASY PULL-OUT ORIGAMI PAPER

Origami patterns by
BRADLEY S. TOMPKINS

ISBN 978-1-4971-0595-9

To learn more about the other great books from Fox Chapel Publishing, or to find a retailer near you, call toll-free at 800-457-9112 or visit us at *www.FoxChapelPublishing.com.*

Or write to:
Fox Chapel Publishing
903 Square Street,
Mount Joy, PA 17552

We are always looking for talented authors.
To submit an idea, please send a brief inquiry to
acquisitions@foxchapelpublishing.com.

Printed in China
First printing

MIX
Paper | Supporting responsible forestry
FSC® C147414

CONTENTS

Origami Symbols

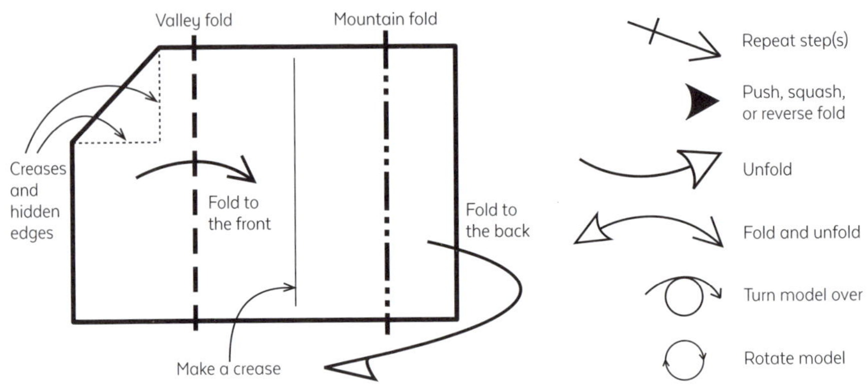

Preliminary Base Instructions

The following base is used as the starting point for the Traditional Crane project on page 13 and the Traditional Star Box on page 17.

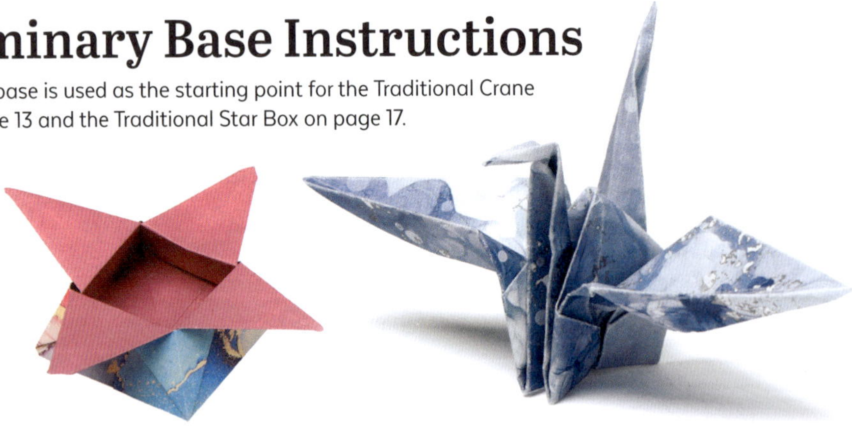

Start with the plain side of the paper facing up. Position the paper like a diamond.

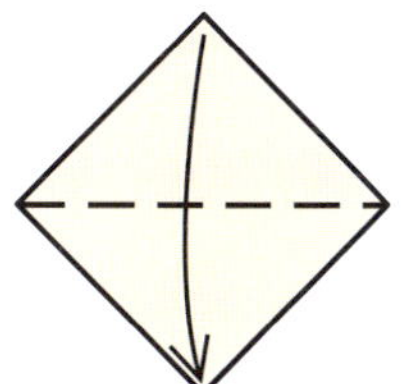

1. Fold the paper in half horizontally, corner to corner.

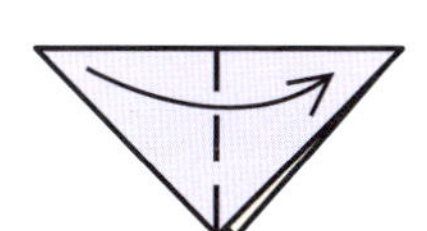

2. Fold the triangle in half vertically.

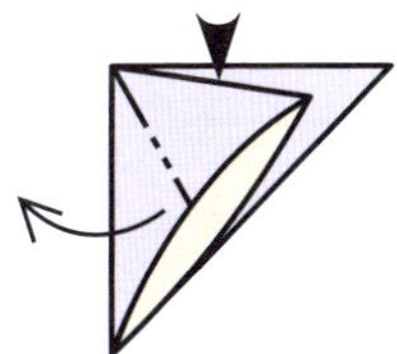

3. Lift the top flap, open it, and squash it flat to form a square.

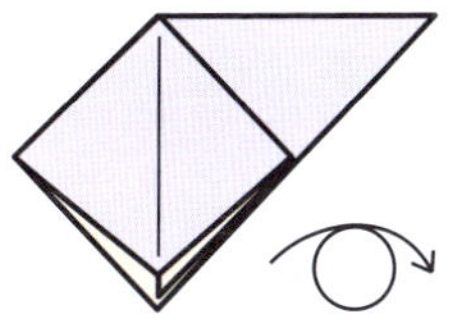

4. Turn the model over.

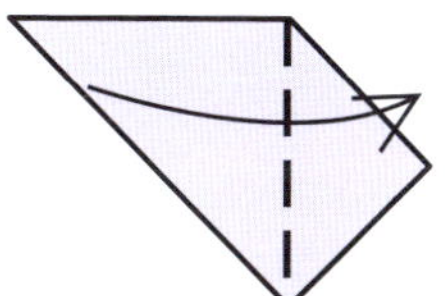

5. Fold over the large flap.

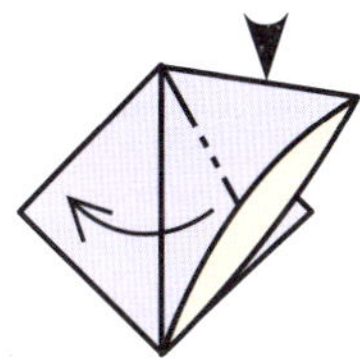

6. Repeat step 3 with the top flap.

Your Preliminary Base is complete.

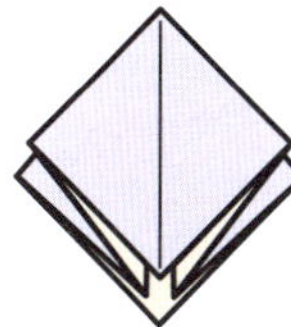

SIMPLE BUTTERFLY

◆

This simple origami butterfly will fly short distances when thrown.

Start with the plain side of the paper facing up. Position the paper like a diamond.

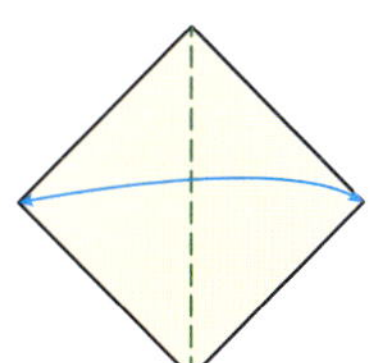

1 Fold the paper in half vertically, corner to corner. Unfold it.

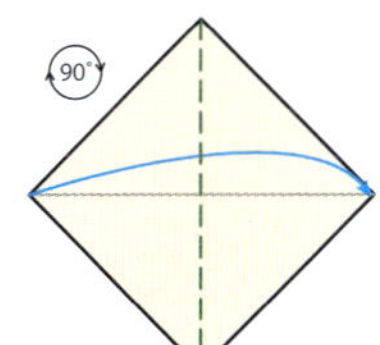

2 Rotate the paper, then fold it in half vertically, corner to corner.

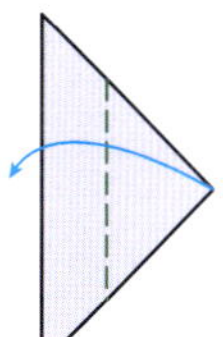

3 Fold back the point of the triangle.

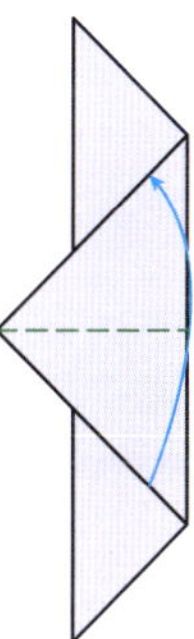

4 Fold the model in half horizontally.

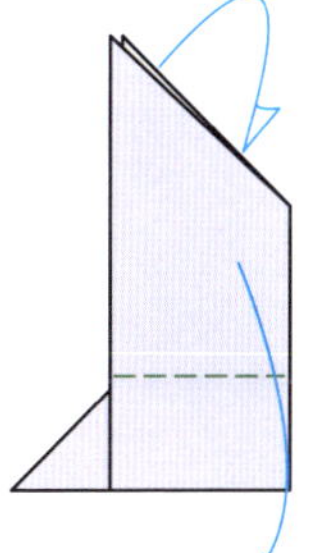

5 Fold the top flap to the front and fold the back flap to the back.

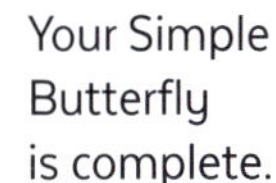

Your Simple Butterfly is complete.

SAILBOAT

This sailboat is an easy practice project. It stands without any support. Happy sailing!

Start with the plain side of the paper facing up. Position the paper like a square.

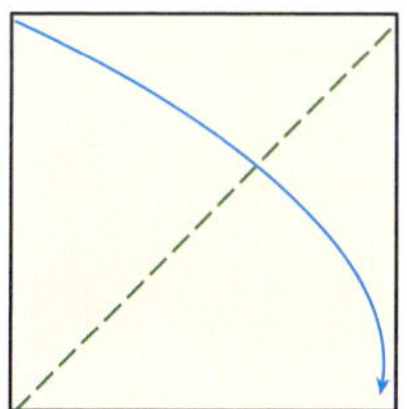

1 Fold the paper in half diagonally, corner to corner.

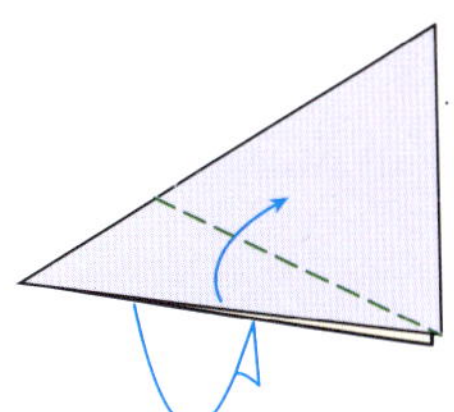

2 Fold up the bottom edge of the model to crease it, then reverse fold along the crease.

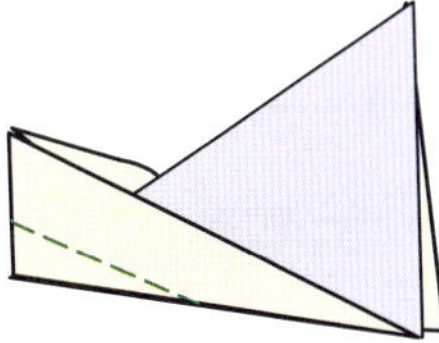

3 Fold up the bottom corner.

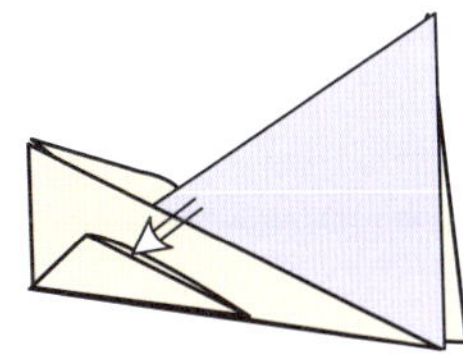

4 Open this corner and squash it flat to form a diamond.

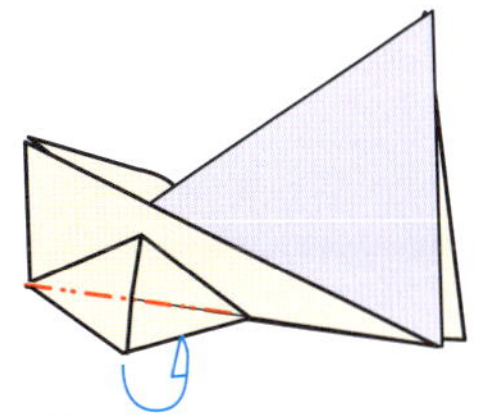

5 Flatten the halves of the base to the front and the back.

Your Simple Boat is complete.

TRADITIONAL BUTTERFLY

This traditional origami butterfly is a graceful design folded from a square of paper, symbolizing transformation, joy, and the beauty of fleeting moments.

Scan the QR code to follow along with the video tutorial.

Start with the plain side of the paper facing up. Position the paper like a square.

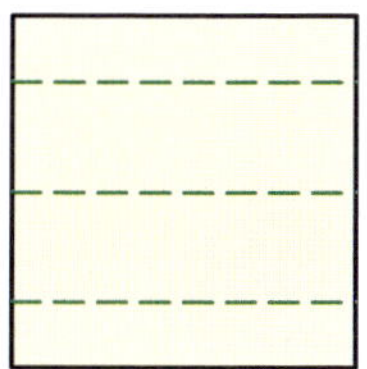

1 Fold the paper in half horizontally, then unfold it. Fold in the top and bottom edges.

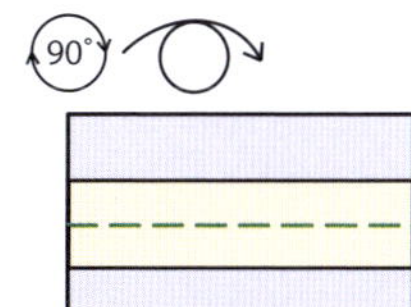

2 Your piece should look like this. Turn it over and rotate it.

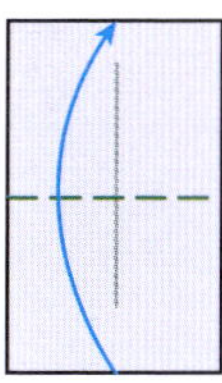

3 Fold the model in half horizontally.

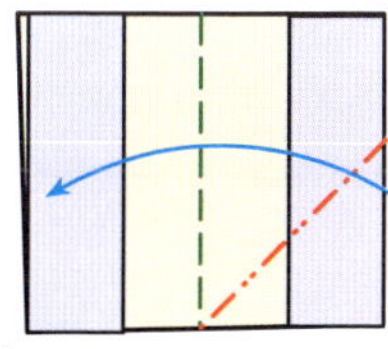

4 Open and squash fold the bottom corner flat to form a triangle.

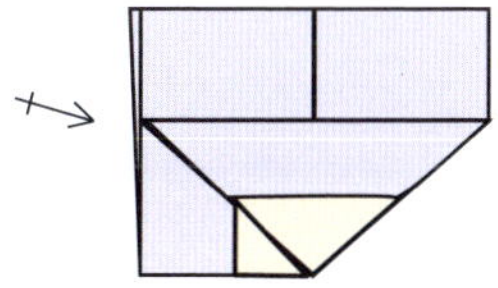

5 Repeat on the other side.

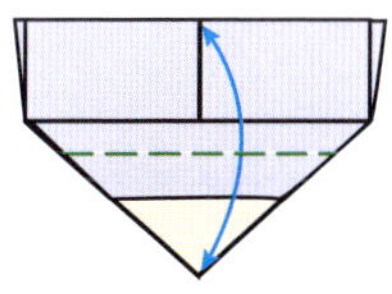

6 Fold the bottom tip up to the top edge, then unfold it.

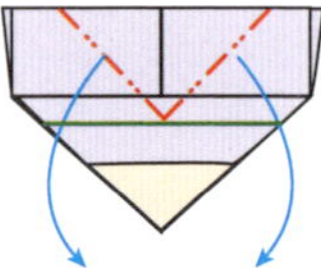

7 Using this line as a guide, squash fold the top layer open to form the wings.

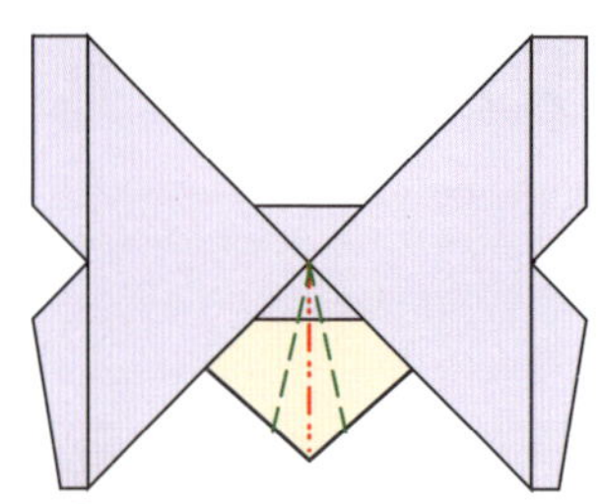

8 Pinch a vertical mountain crease in the center of the body. Make two angled valley creases on either side.

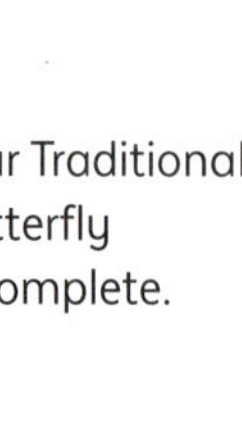

Your Traditional Butterfly is complete.

TRADITIONAL CRANE

The traditional origami crane is a graceful bird folded from a single square of paper, often representing peace, hope, and long life in Japanese culture.

Scan the QR code to follow along with the video tutorial.

Start with a Preliminary Base (see page 4). Position the closed point at the top.

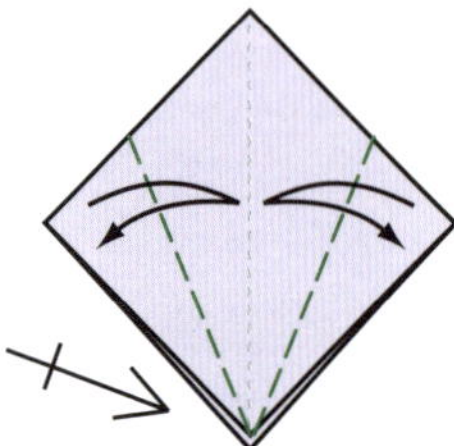

1 Fold the top flaps into the center line, then unfold them. Repeat on the other side.

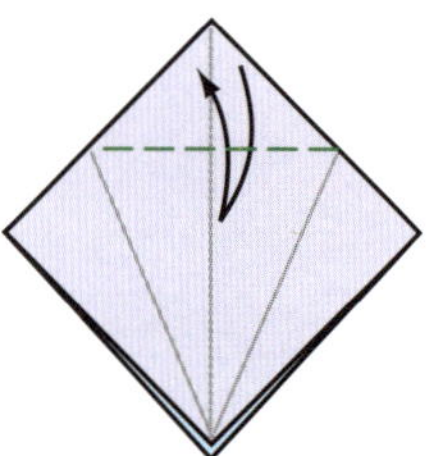

2 Fold down the top point, then unfold it.

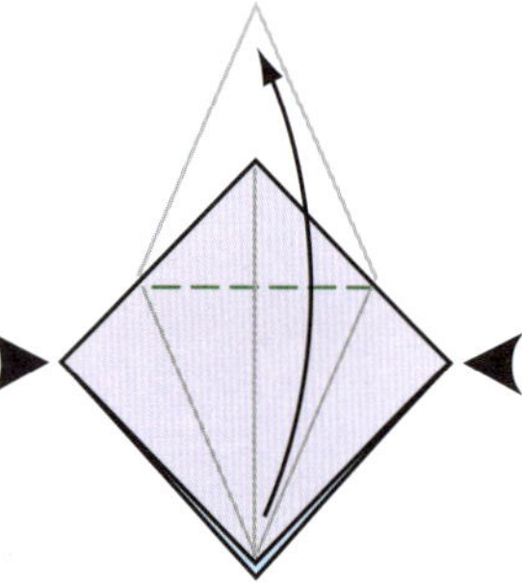

3 Lift and open the top flap and begin to press it flat.

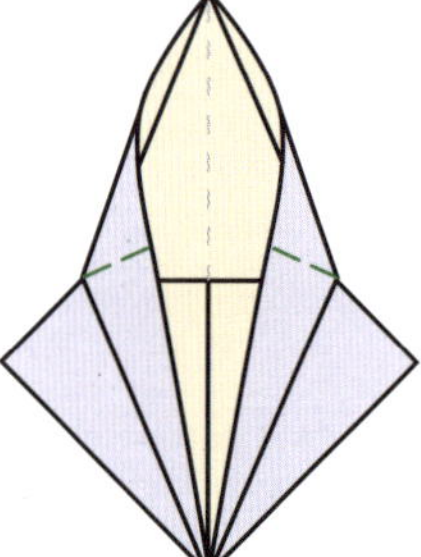

4 Continue pressing this layer flat.

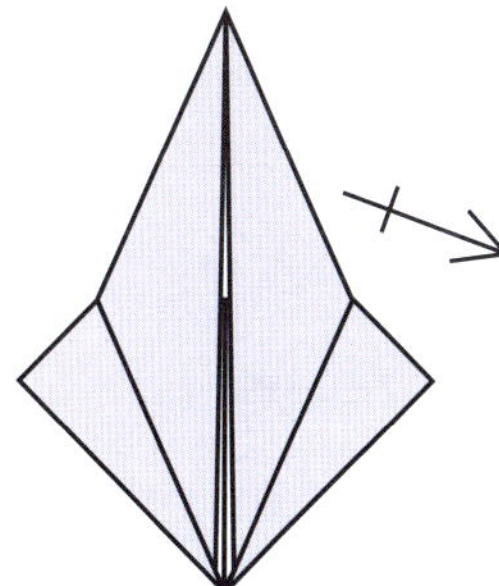

5 The model should look like this. Turn the model over and repeat steps 3–4.

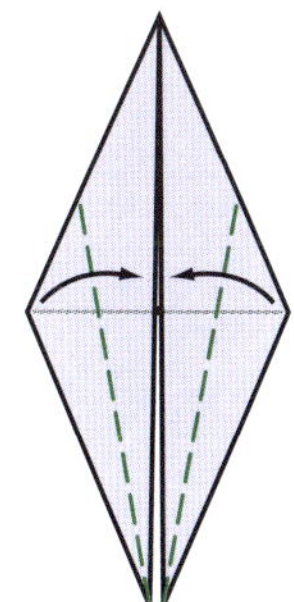

6 Fold the top flaps into the centerline.

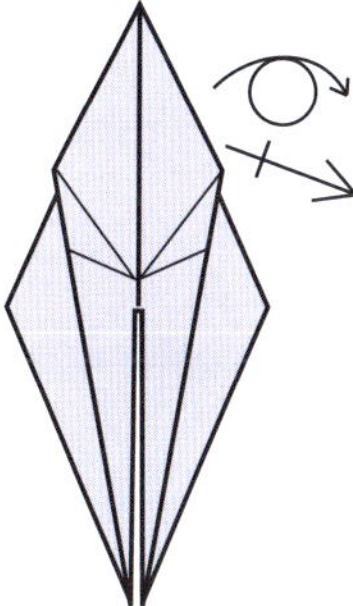

7 The model should look like this. Turn the model over and repeat step 6.

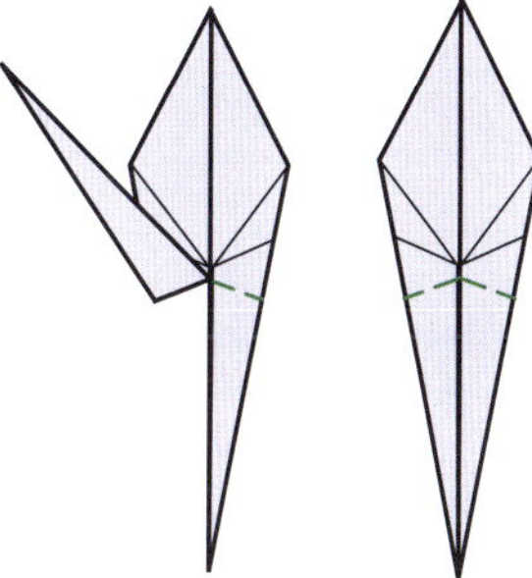

8 Fold the bottom points up at an angle, then unfold them.

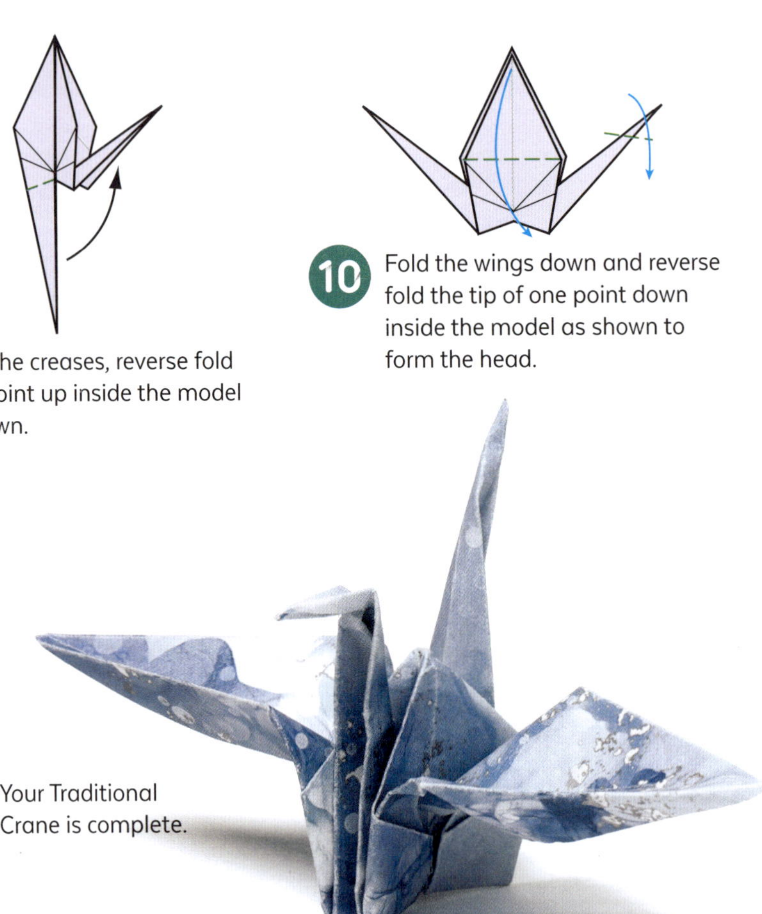

9 Using the creases, reverse fold each point up inside the model as shown.

10 Fold the wings down and reverse fold the tip of one point down inside the model as shown to form the head.

Your Traditional Crane is complete.

STAR BOX

This popular tutorial box is great for beginners.

Scan the QR code to follow along with the video tutorial.

Start with a Preliminary Base (see page 4). Position the closed point at the bottom.

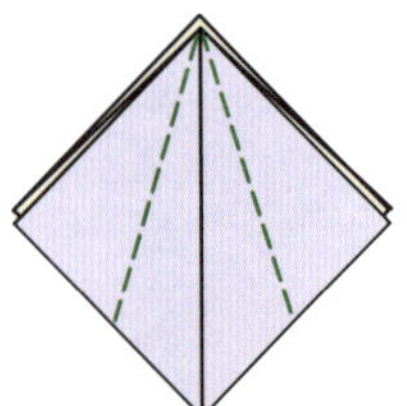

1. Fold the top flaps into the centerline.

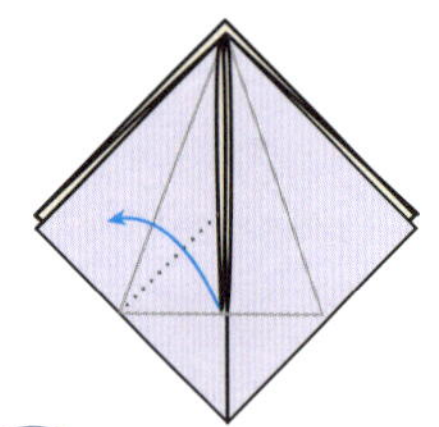

2. Open and flatten the left flap.

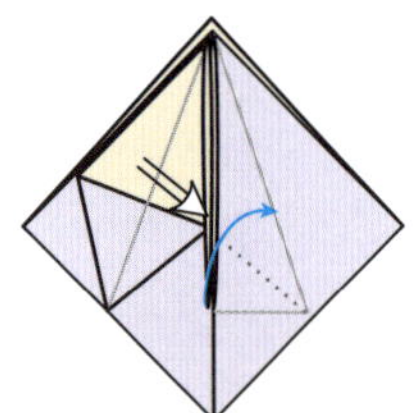

3. Repeat with the right flap.

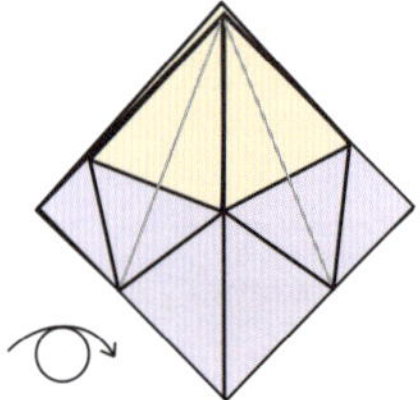

4. Your model should look like this. Turn the model over and repeat steps 1–3.

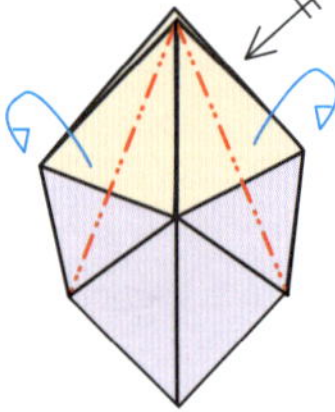

5. Fold the edges of the top flaps back into the center of the model. Repeat on the other side.

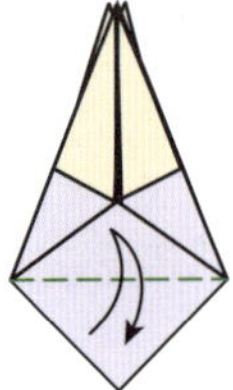

6. Fold the bottom point up, then unfold it.

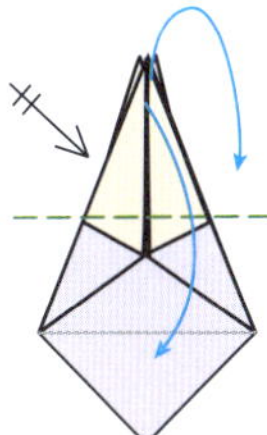

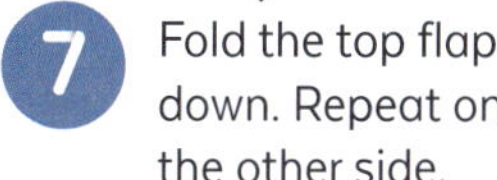

7 Fold the top flap down. Repeat on the other side.

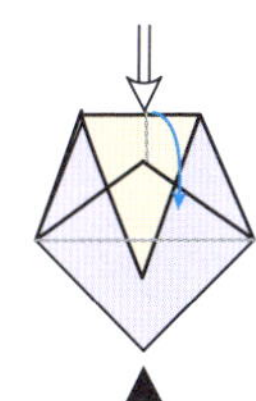

8 Pull the flaps apart and fold down the remaining two flaps. Flatten the bottom.

Your Star Box is complete.

RYE BOX

This box has beautiful petal details. Try starting your folds with the design facing up to create a different look.

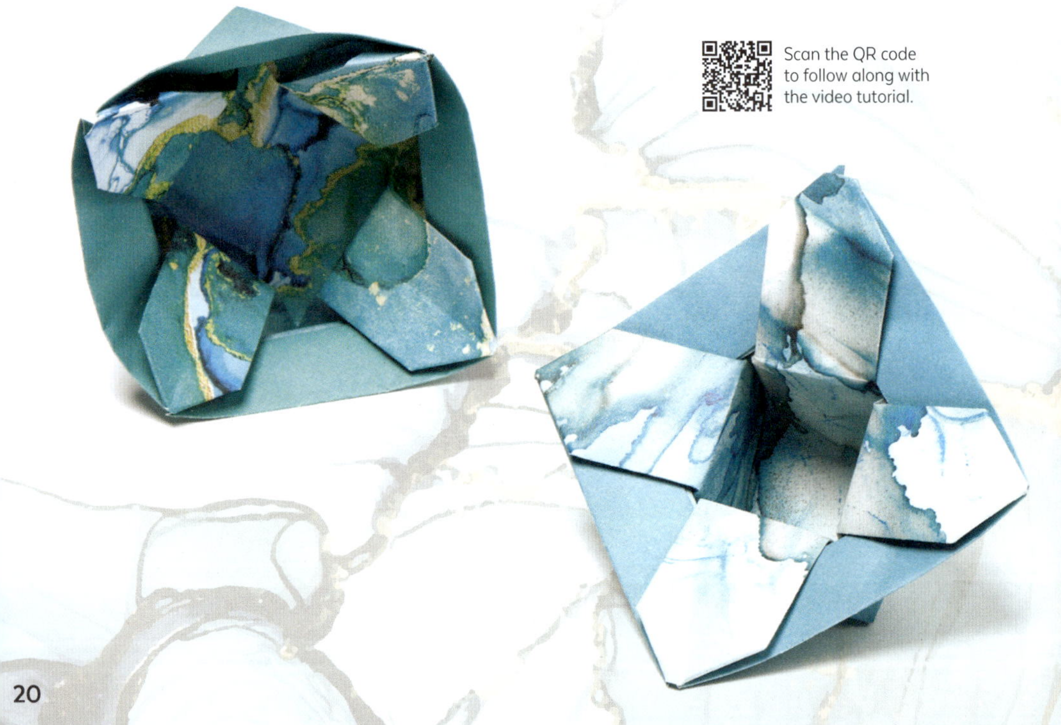

Scan the QR code to follow along with the video tutorial.

Start with the plain side of the paper facing up. Position the paper like a square.

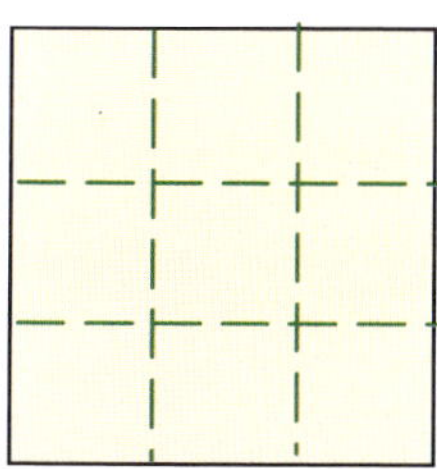

1 Valley fold the paper horizontally and vertically into thirds, then unfold it.

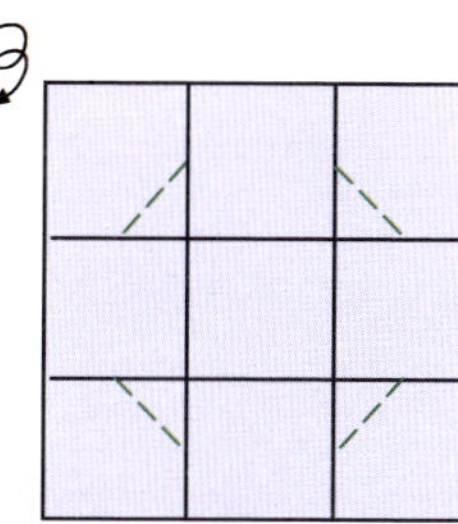

2 Turn the model over. Fold the corners into the center, then unfold them. Crease only where shown.

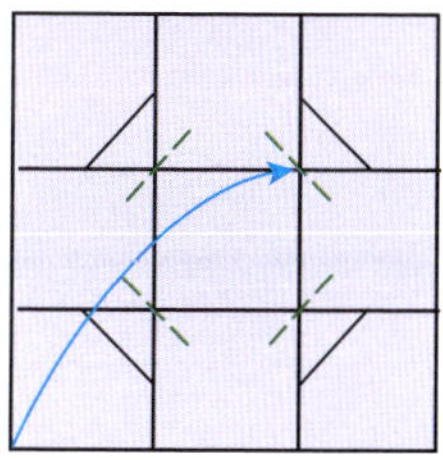

3 Fold the corners to the opposite third, then unfold them. Crease only where shown.

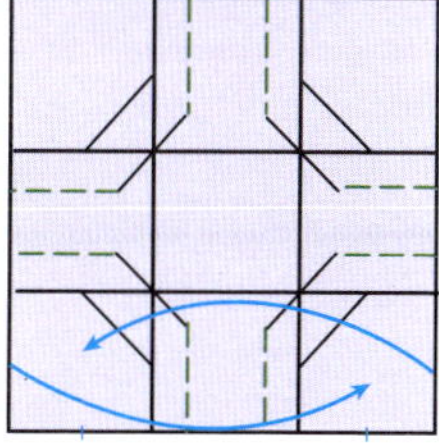

4 Fold the edges to the centers of the opposite thirds, then unfold them. Crease only where shown.

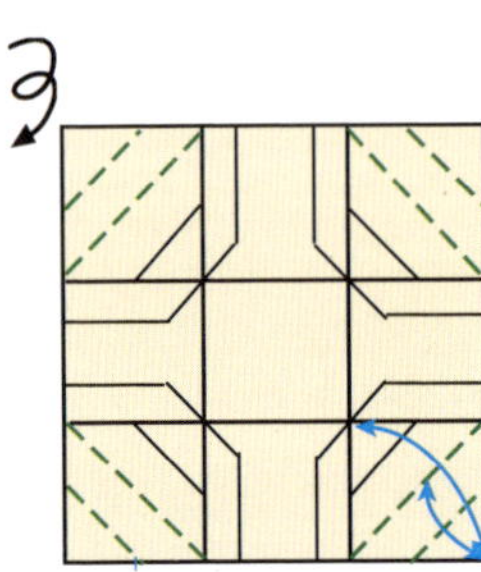

5 Turn the model over. Fold the corner thirds in half, then unfold them. Fold the corners to these diagonals, then fold them over again.

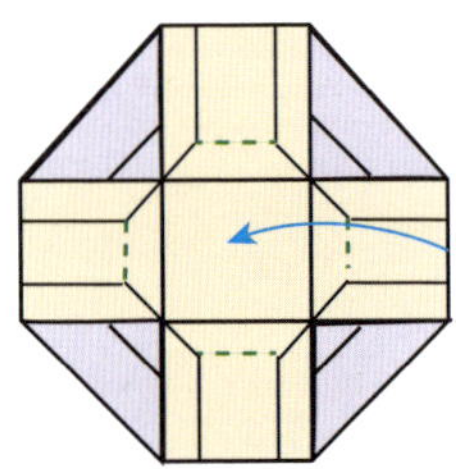

6 Fold the edges into the center, then unfold them. Crease only where shown.

7 Push the folded-over corners into the center while mountain folding them to collapse the box.

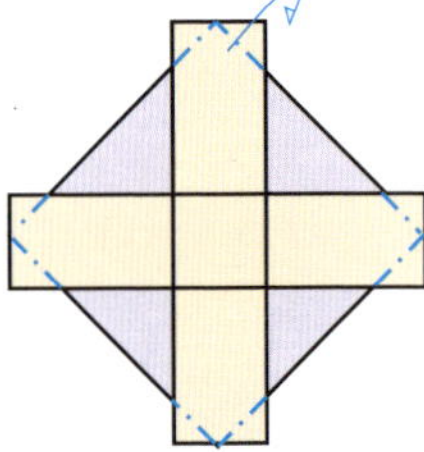

8 Fold each corner flap in and under itself to secure the model.

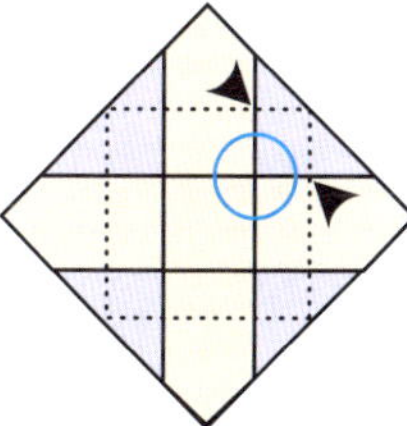

9 Grasp the model where shown and pinch together the creases on the bottom of the box below. Repeat with each corner.

Your Rye Box is complete.

ANTONY BOX

This little package is the perfect secret keeper.

Scan the QR code to follow along with the video tutorial.

Start with the patterned side of the paper facing up. Position the paper like a square.

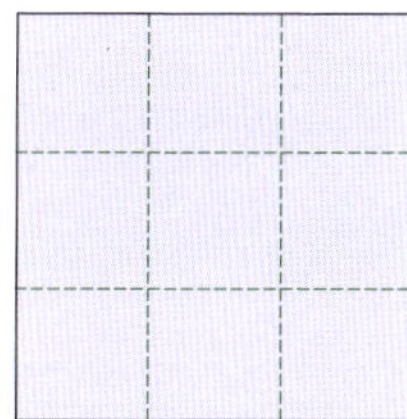

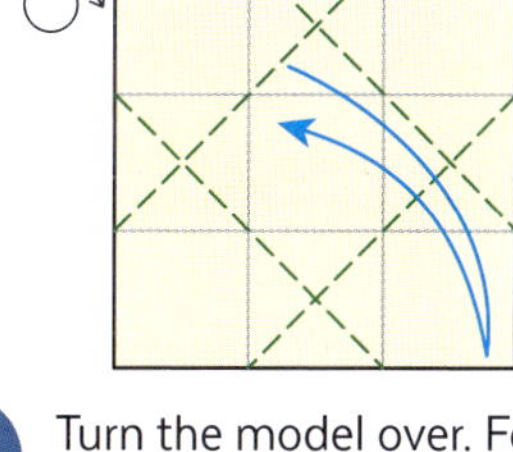

1 Valley fold the paper horizontally and vertically into thirds, then unfold it.

2 Turn the model over. Fold the corners into the opposite third, then unfold them.

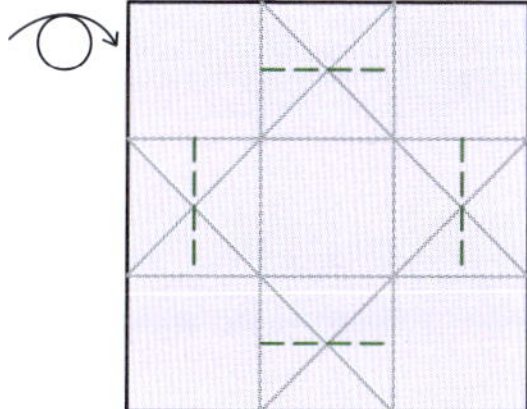

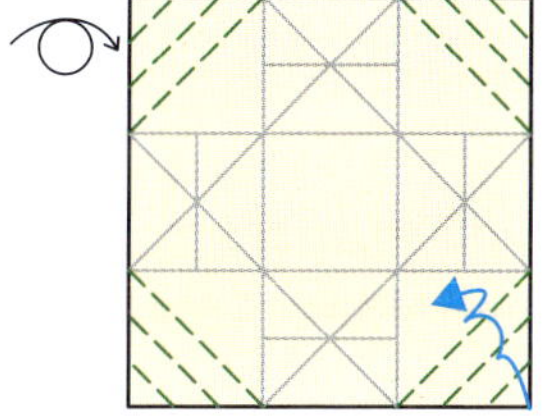

3 Turn the model over. Fold the edges into the nearest third line, then unfold them. Crease only where shown.

4 Turn the model over. Fold the corner squares in half diagonally, then unfold them. Fold the outer triangles over three times as shown to create thin bands.

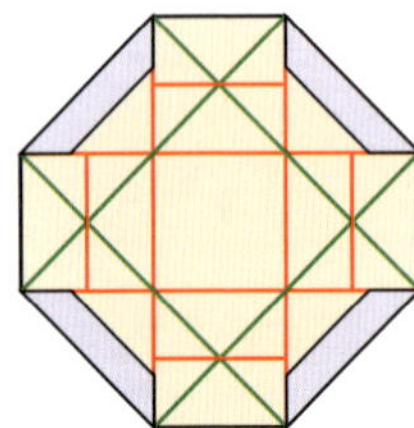

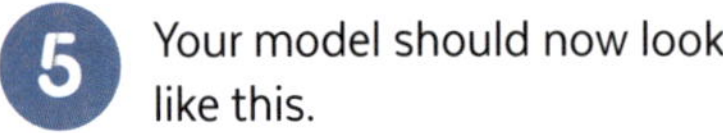

5 Your model should now look like this.

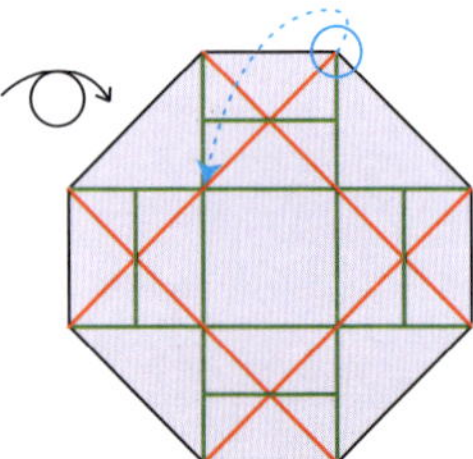

6 Turn the model over. Fold back the top corner to match the opposite bottom corner.

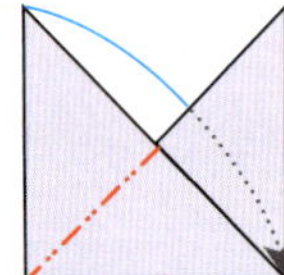

7 Repeat with the other corner of the square. Repeat with the remaining squares. The bands should overlap.

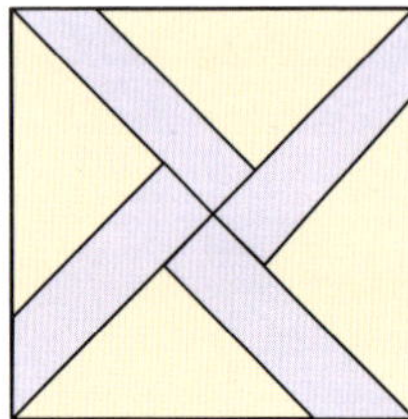

8 Tuck each band under the band next to it, like closing a cardboard box.

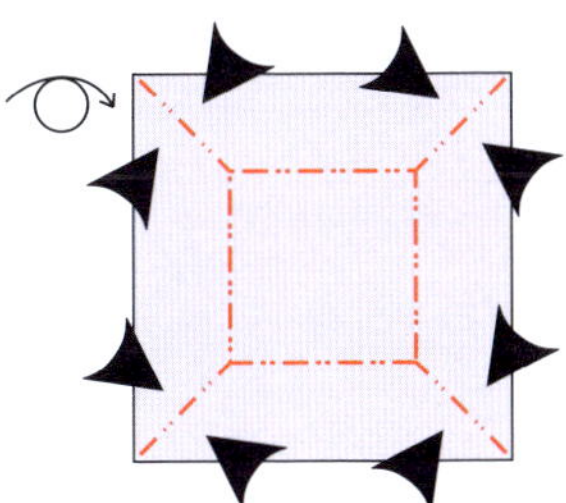

9 Turn the model over. Squeeze the bottom layer at each corner to shape the box.

Your Antony Box is complete.

TAURUS BOX

This unusual box has sharp points like the horns of a bull.

Start with the plain side of the paper facing up. Position the paper like a square.

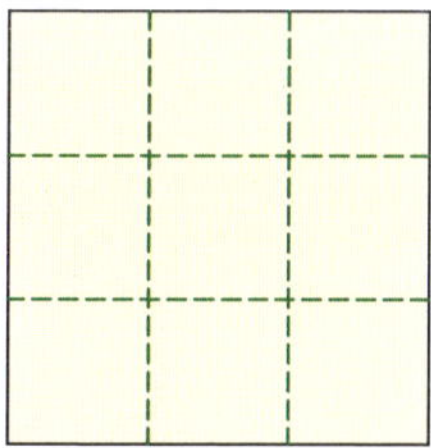

1 Valley fold the paper horizontally and vertically into thirds, then unfold it.

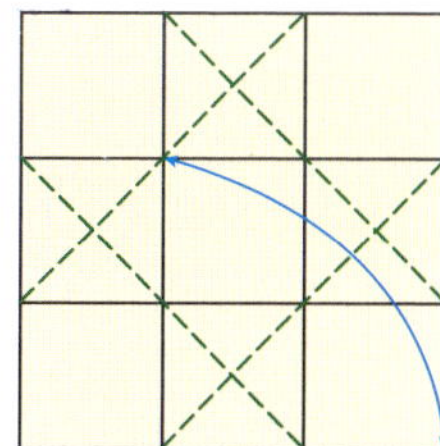

2 Fold the corners into the opposite third, then unfold them.

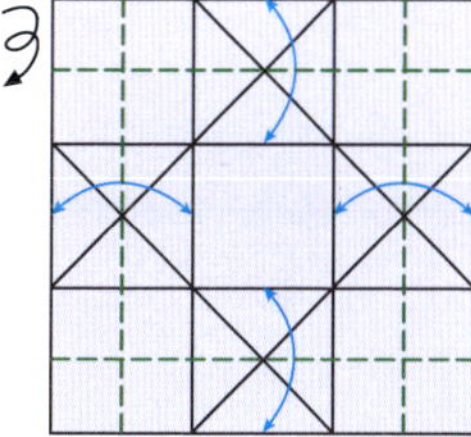

3 Turn the model over. Fold the edges into the nearest third line, then unfold them.

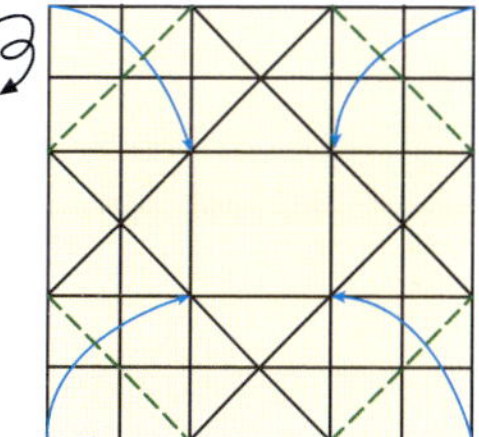

4 Turn the model over. Fold the corner squares in half diagonally.

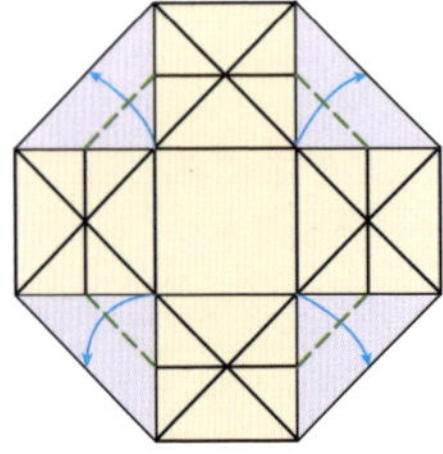

5 Fold the tip of each triangle back to the outer edge.

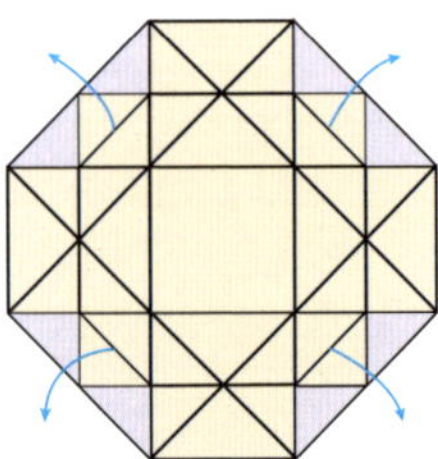

6 Open the model, leaving only the outer triangles folded.

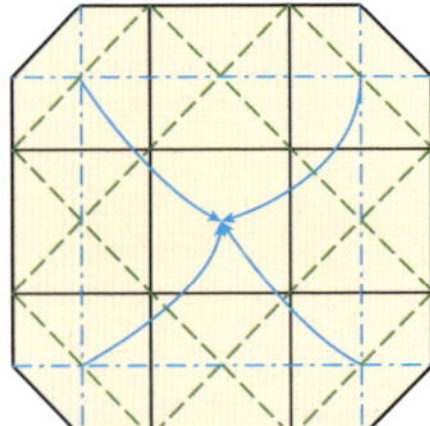

7 Using the creases, fold the outer points into the center to collapse the shape. Work each corner separately.

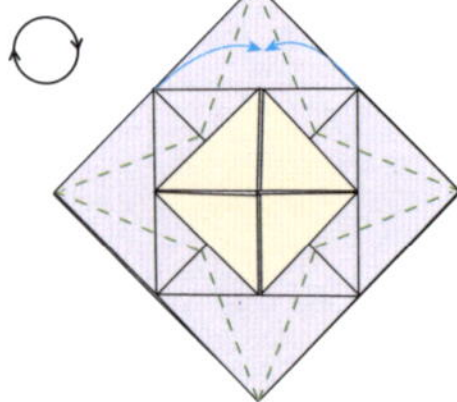

8 Rotate the model. Fold all the outer tabs over the center section.

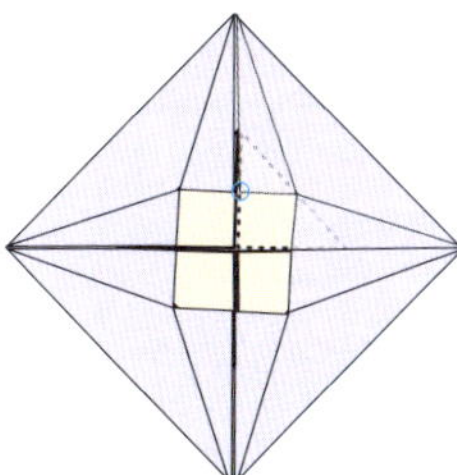

9 Tuck the folded-over corners beneath the triangles of the center section.

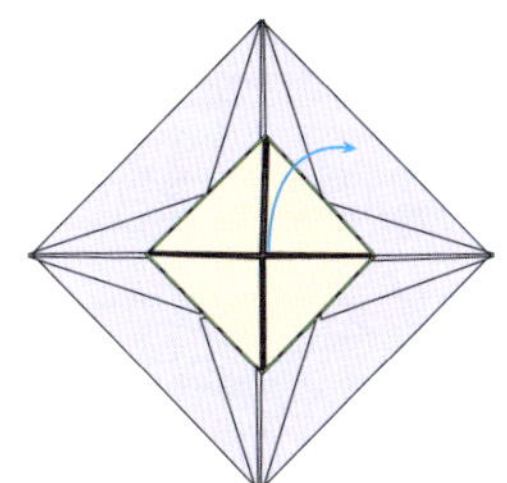

10 Fold the points of the center triangles back to the outer edge.

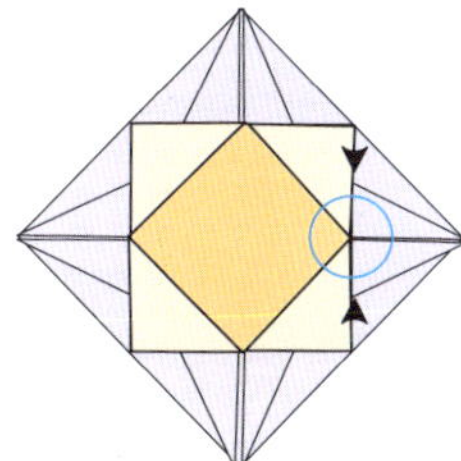

11 Grasp the model where shown and pinch together the corners to expand the box. Repeat with each corner.

Your Taurus Box is complete.

MERRIDY BOX

This box pulls together vintage art deco shapes to create a gorgeous finished piece.

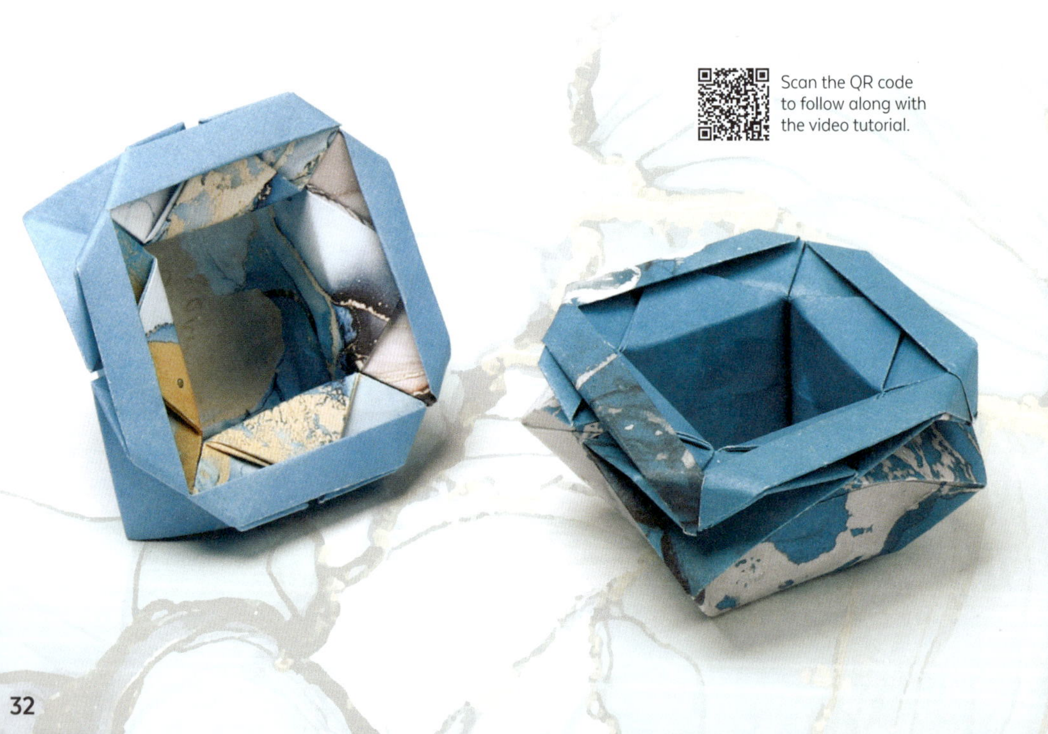

Scan the QR code to follow along with the video tutorial.

Start with the patterned side of the paper facing up. Position the paper like a square.

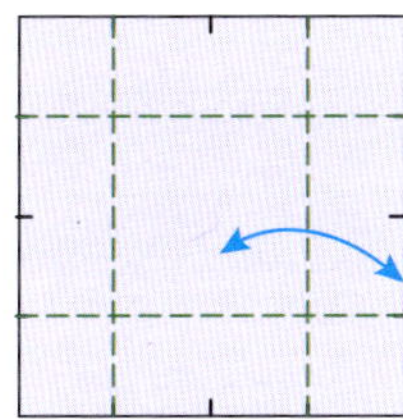

1 Fold the edges into the center. Unfold them.

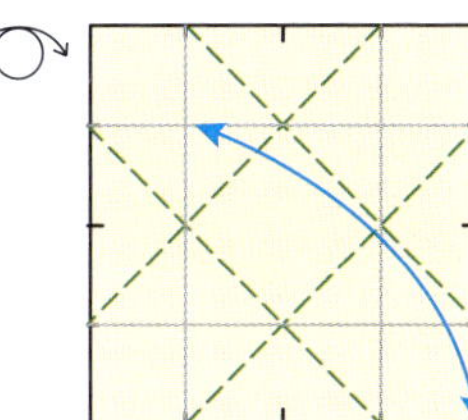

2 Turn the paper over. Fold the corners to the opposite intersection points. Unfold them.

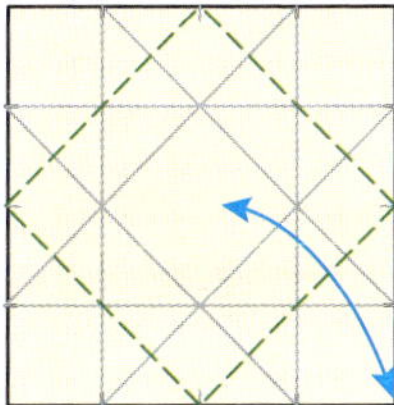

3 Fold the corners into the center. Unfold them.

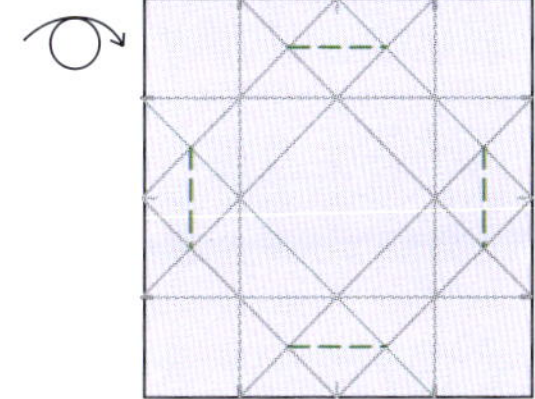

4 Turn the paper over. Fold over the outer diamond shapes, then unfold them. Crease only where shown.

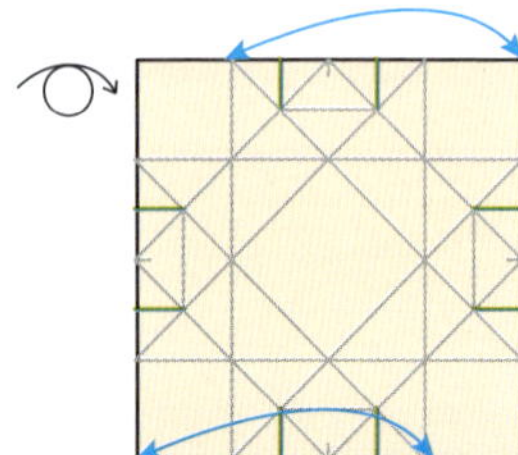

5 Turn the paper over. Fold the outer edges to the opposite fold line, then unfold them. Crease only where shown.

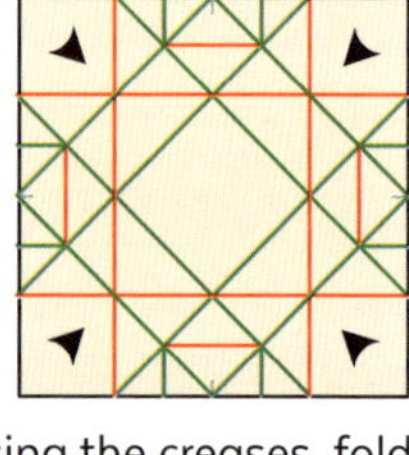

6 Using the creases, fold the outer squares into the center to collapse the shape. Work each corner separately.

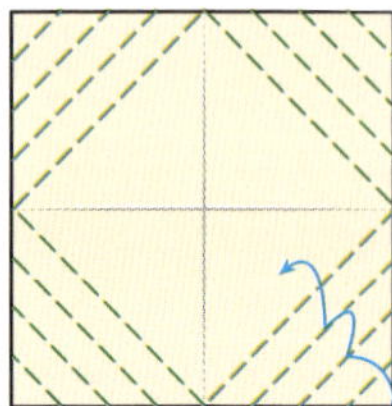

7 Your model will now be a smaller square made of four squares. Fold the corners into the center, then in half, then in quarters to create creases. Fold over each to create thin bands.

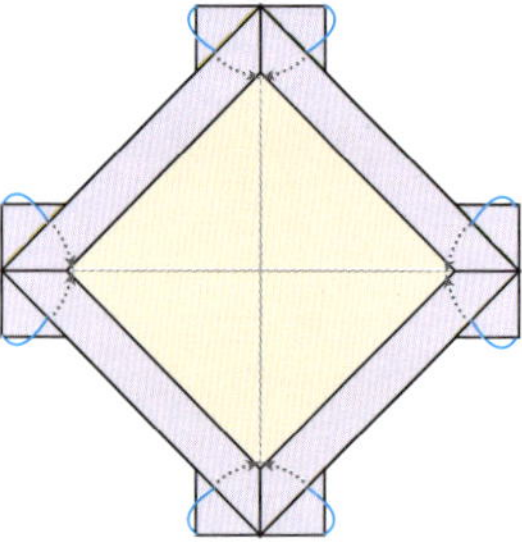

8 Tuck the corners beneath the rims.

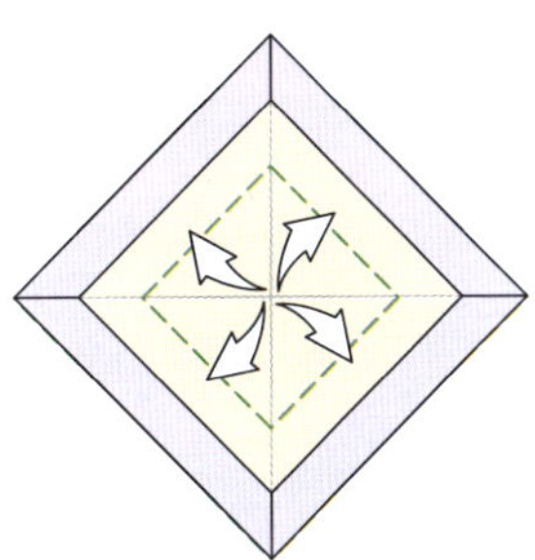

9 Tuck the points of the center triangles back beneath the rims.

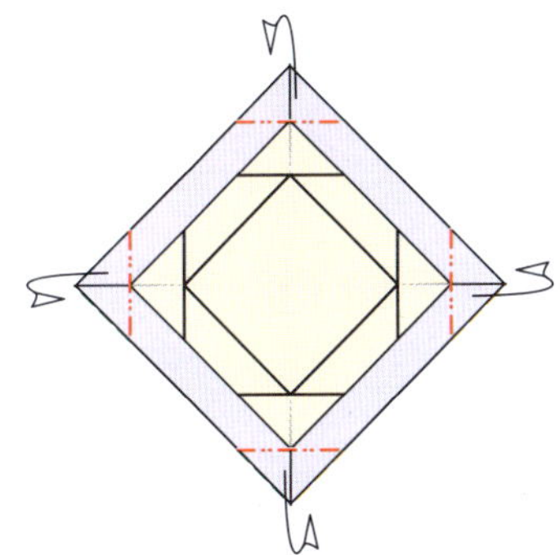

10 Fold the top corners under to lock the shape in place.

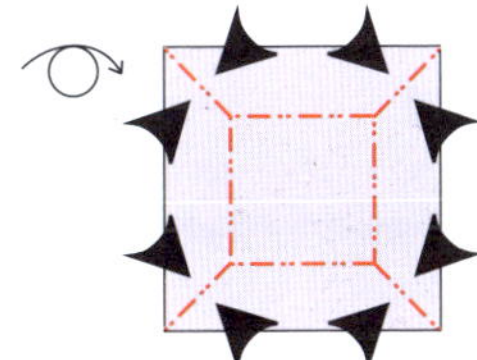

11 Turn the model over. Pinch the corners of the bottom layer together to expand the box.

Your Merridy Box is complete.

ELENDIL BOX

This box is customizable—you can leave the top flat to create a closed package, or fold the pieces back to create something that looks a bit more decorative.

Scan the QR code to follow along with the video tutorial.

Start with the patterned side of the paper facing up. Position the paper like a square.

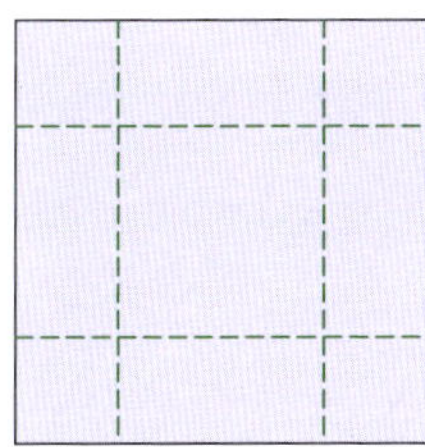

1. Fold the edges into the center. Unfold them.

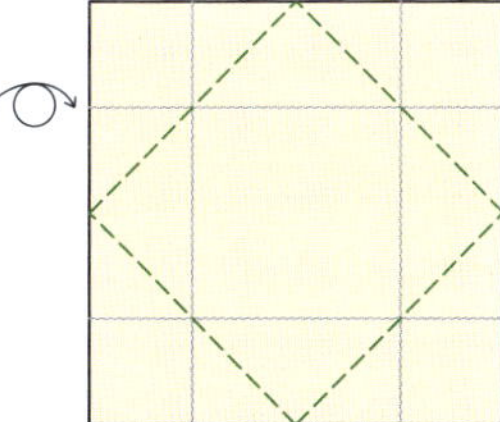

2. Turn the paper over. Fold the corners into the center. Unfold them.

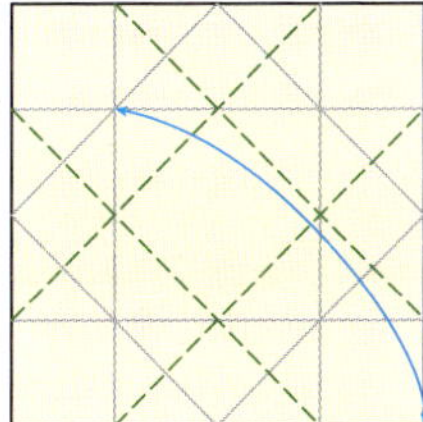

3. Fold the corners to the opposite intersection points. Unfold them.

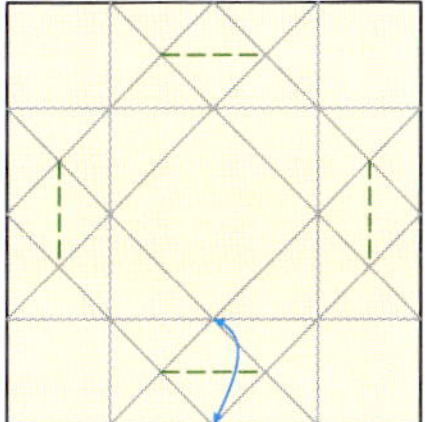

4. Fold over the outer diamond shapes, then unfold them. Crease only where shown.

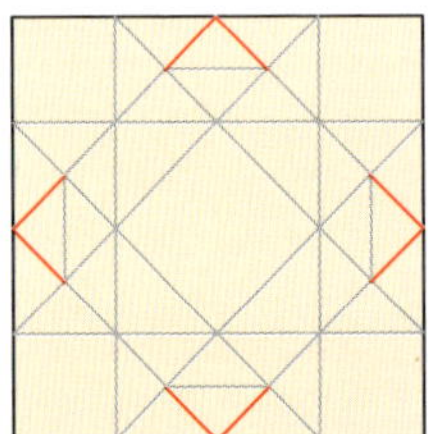

5 Refold the creases marked in red as mountain folds.

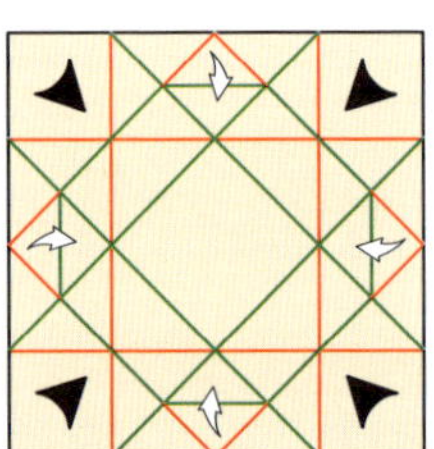

6 Using the creases, fold the outer squares into the center to collapse the shape. Work each corner separately.

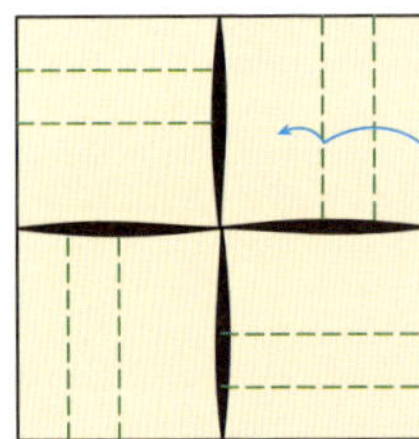

7 Your model will now be a smaller square made of four squares. Fold the edges in as shown to create thin bands.

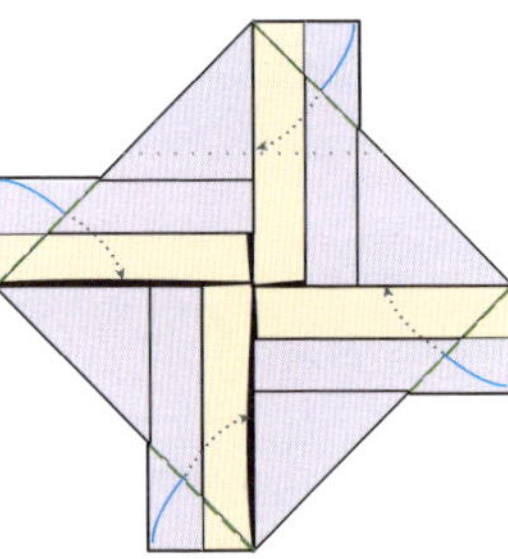

8 Tuck the corners of the bands in underneath the bands.

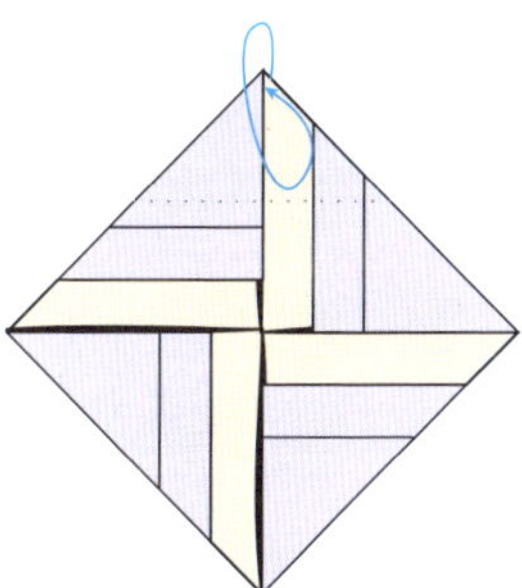

9 Tuck the folded-over points of the bands into the corner pockets.

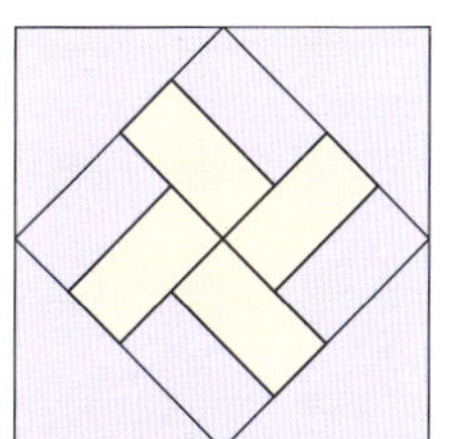

10 Your model should look like this. Fold back the center flaps to create an opening.

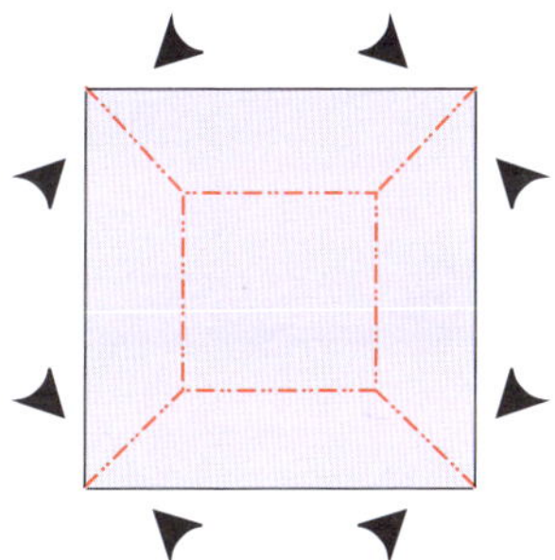

11 Turn the model over. Pinch the corners of the bottom layer together to expand the box.

Your Elendil Box is complete.

The following section includes a rainbow of colorful origami papers, featuring gorgeous alcohol ink designs with complementary colors. The sheets are perforated, so you can easily remove them and start folding your own beautiful pieces of paper art.

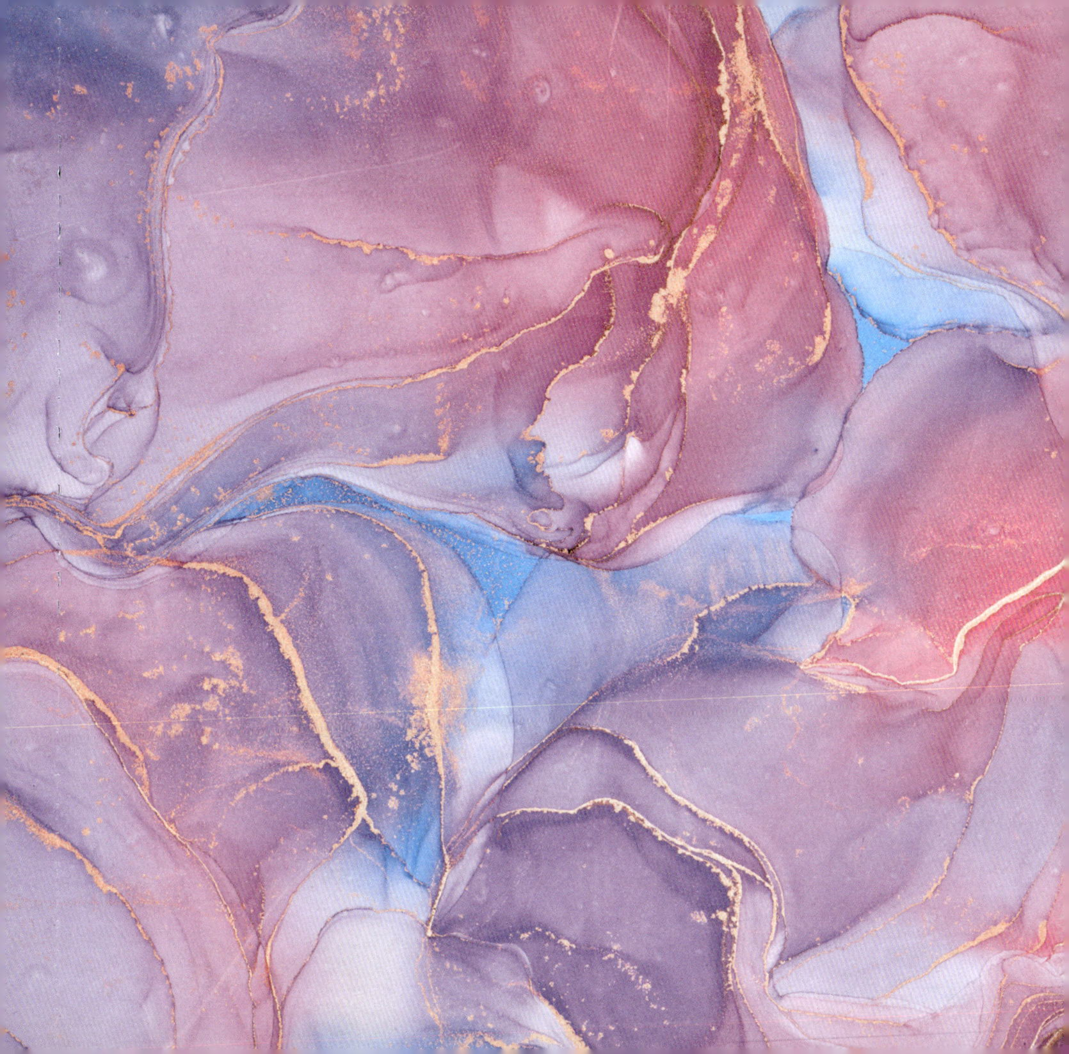

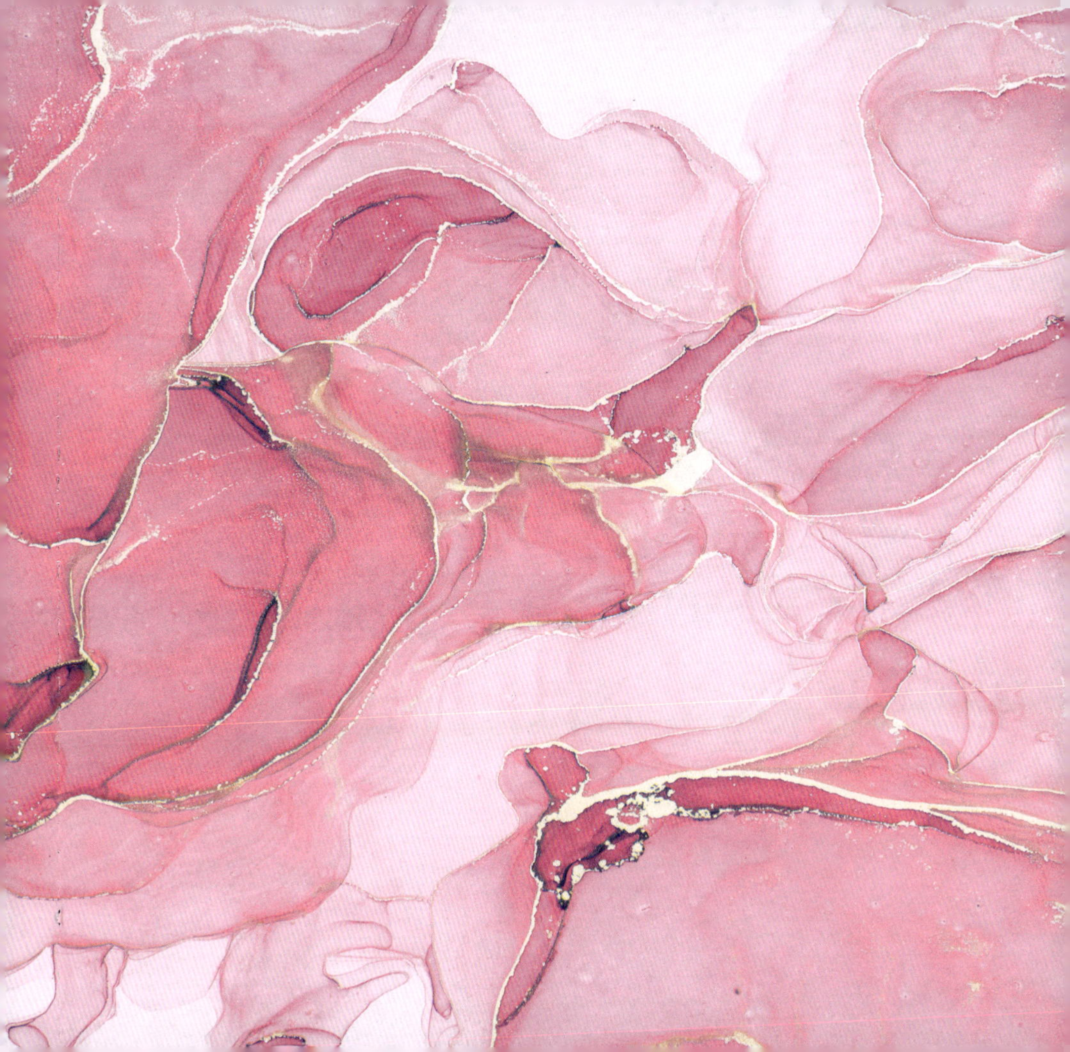

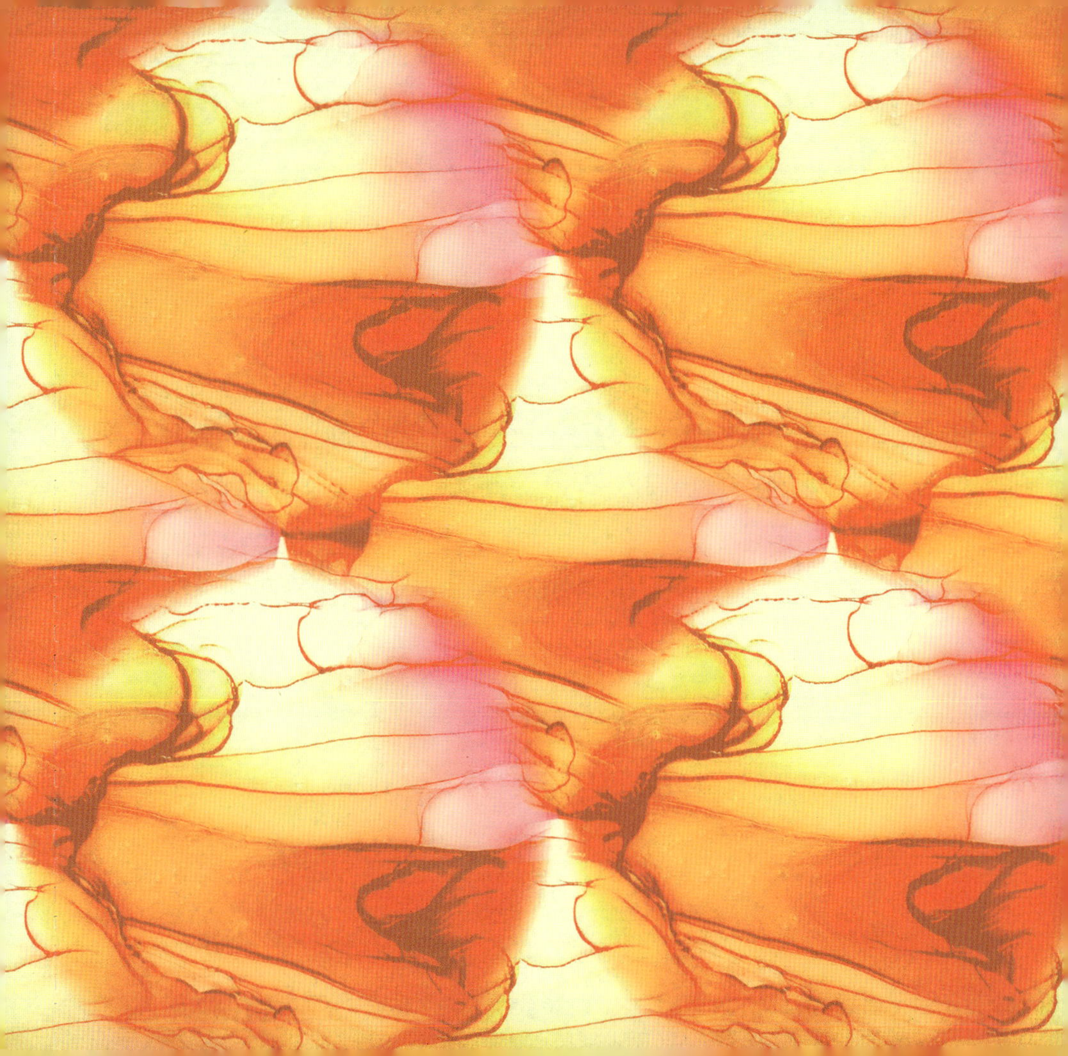

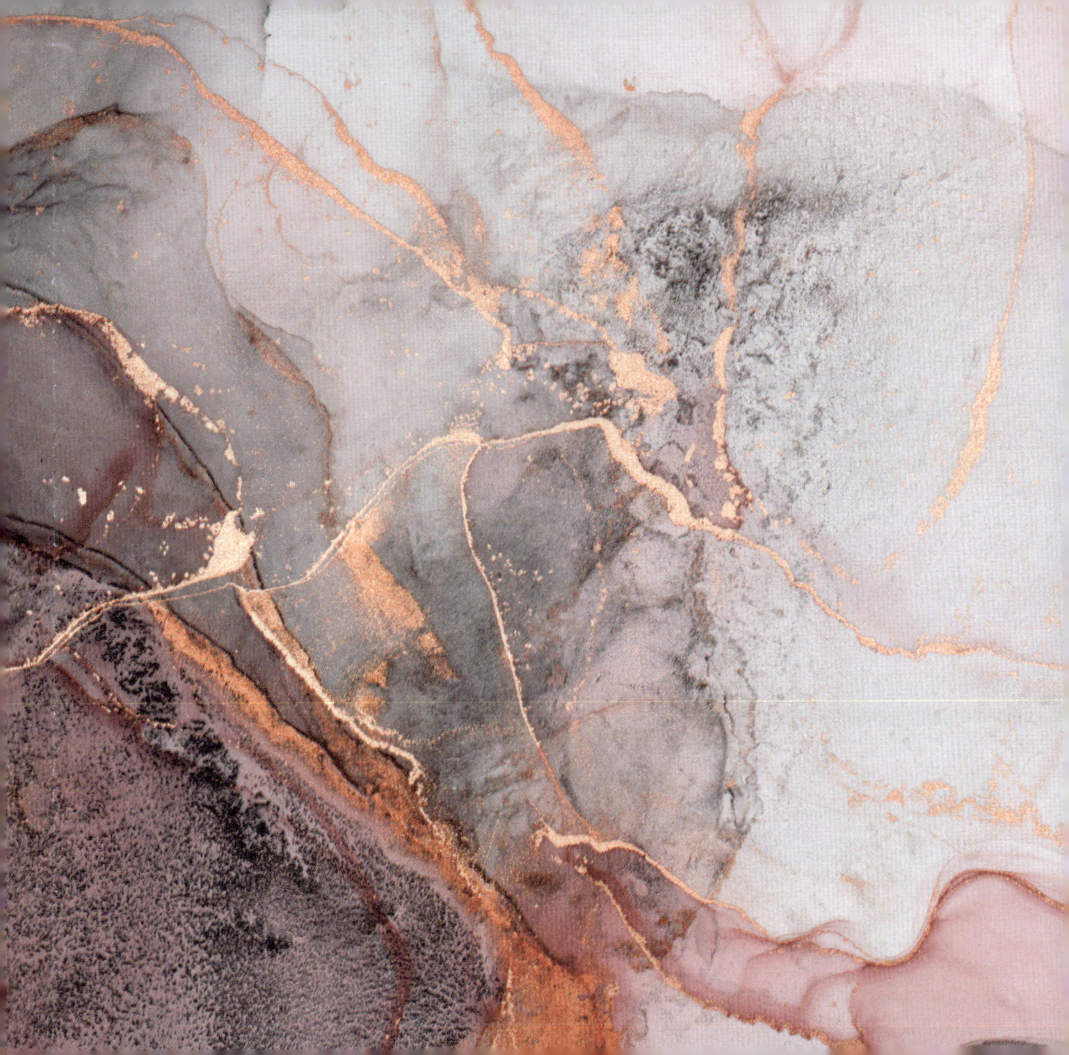

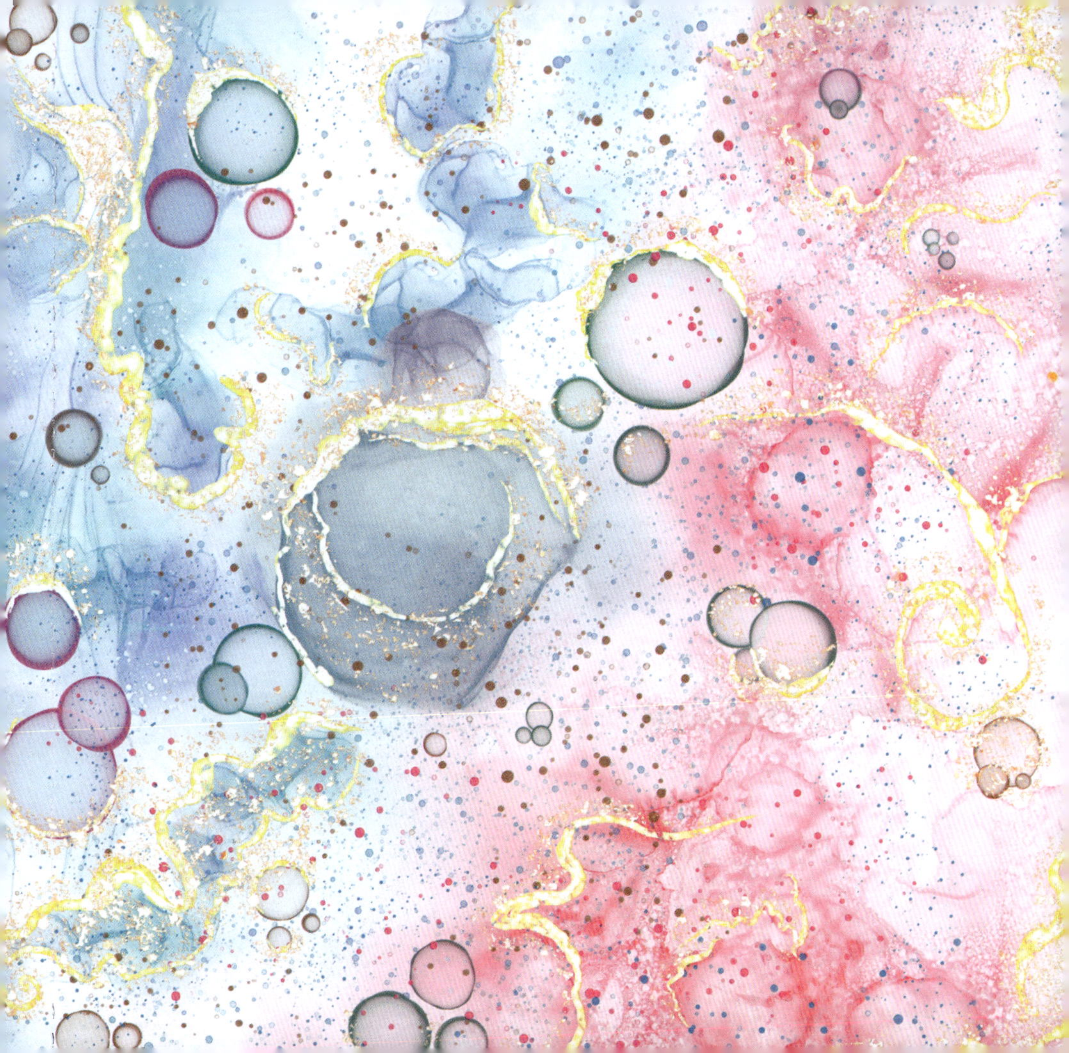

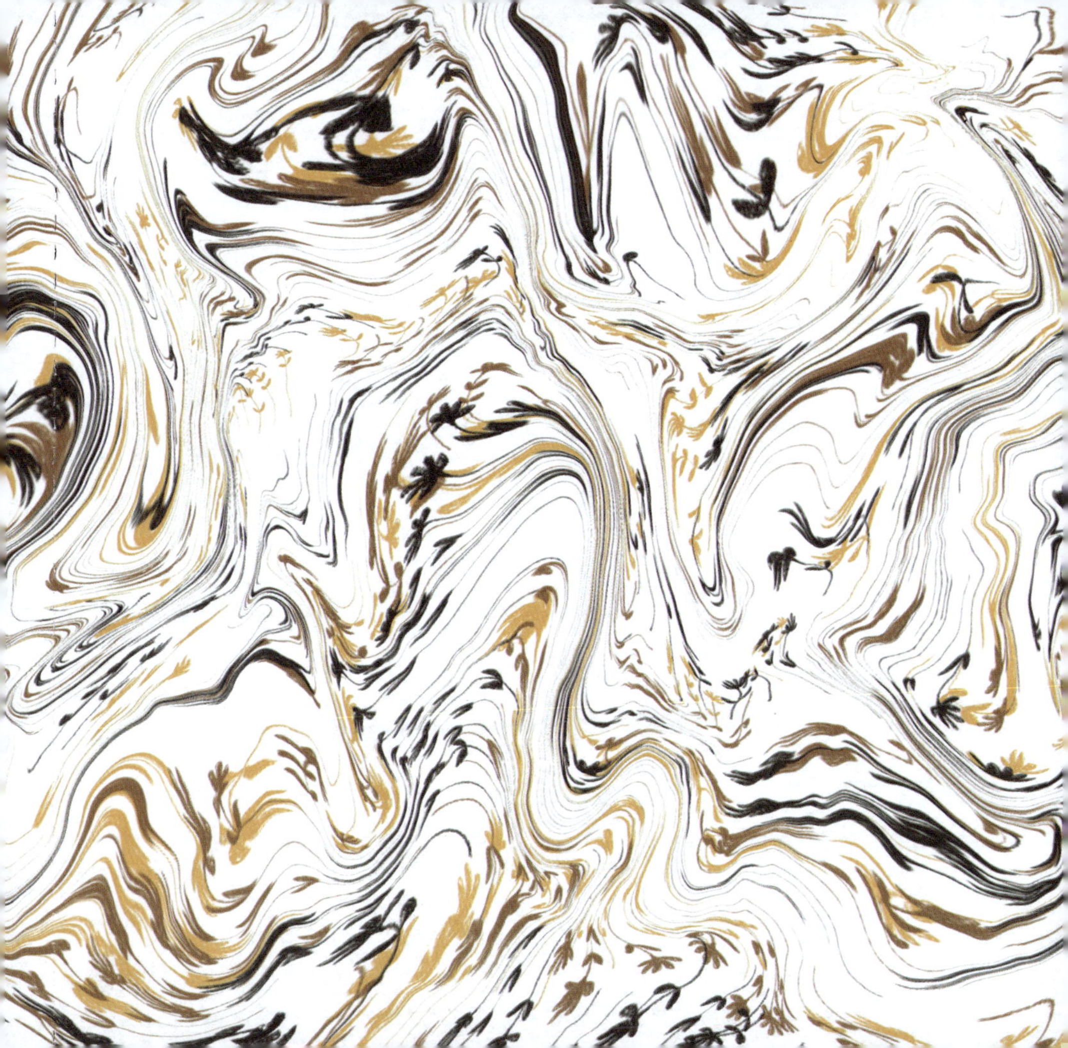

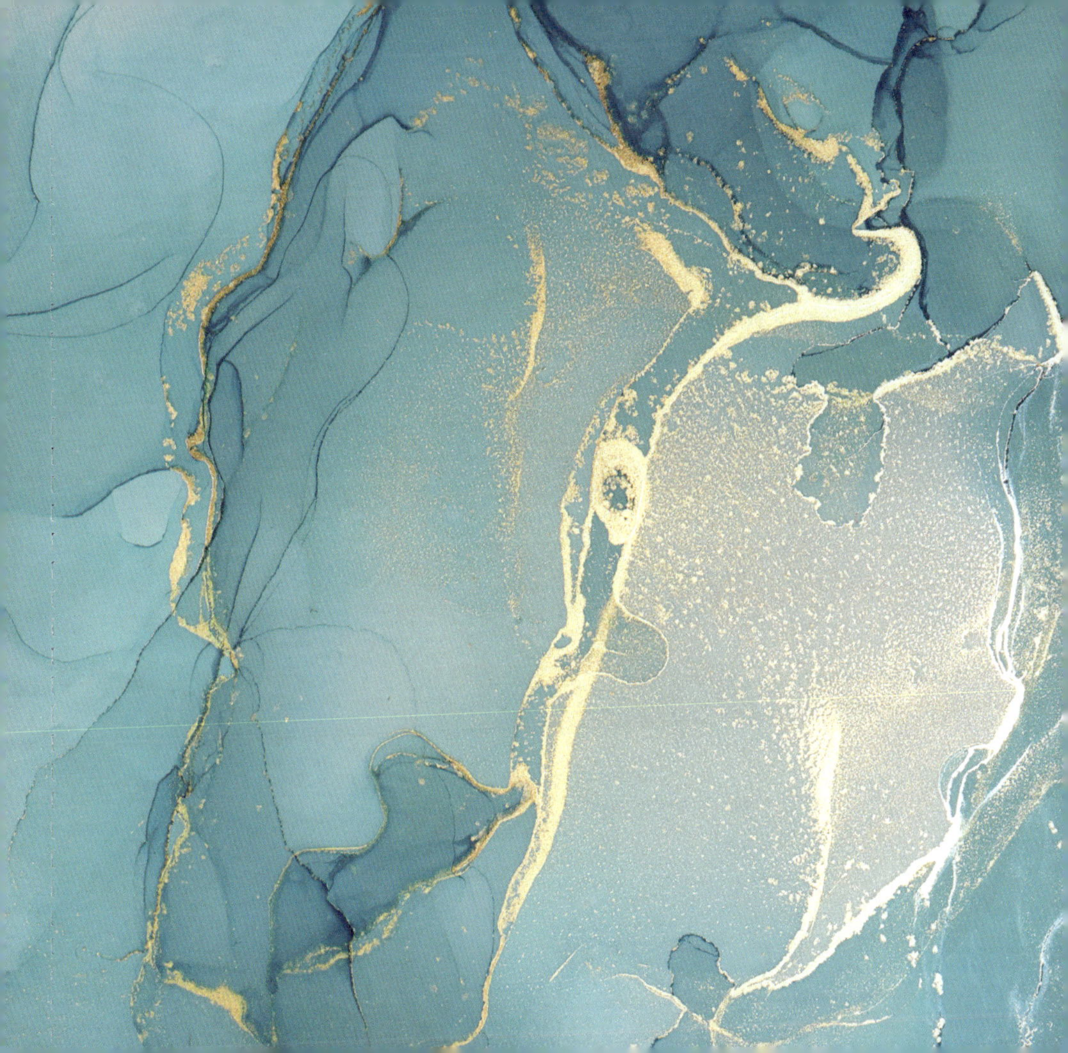

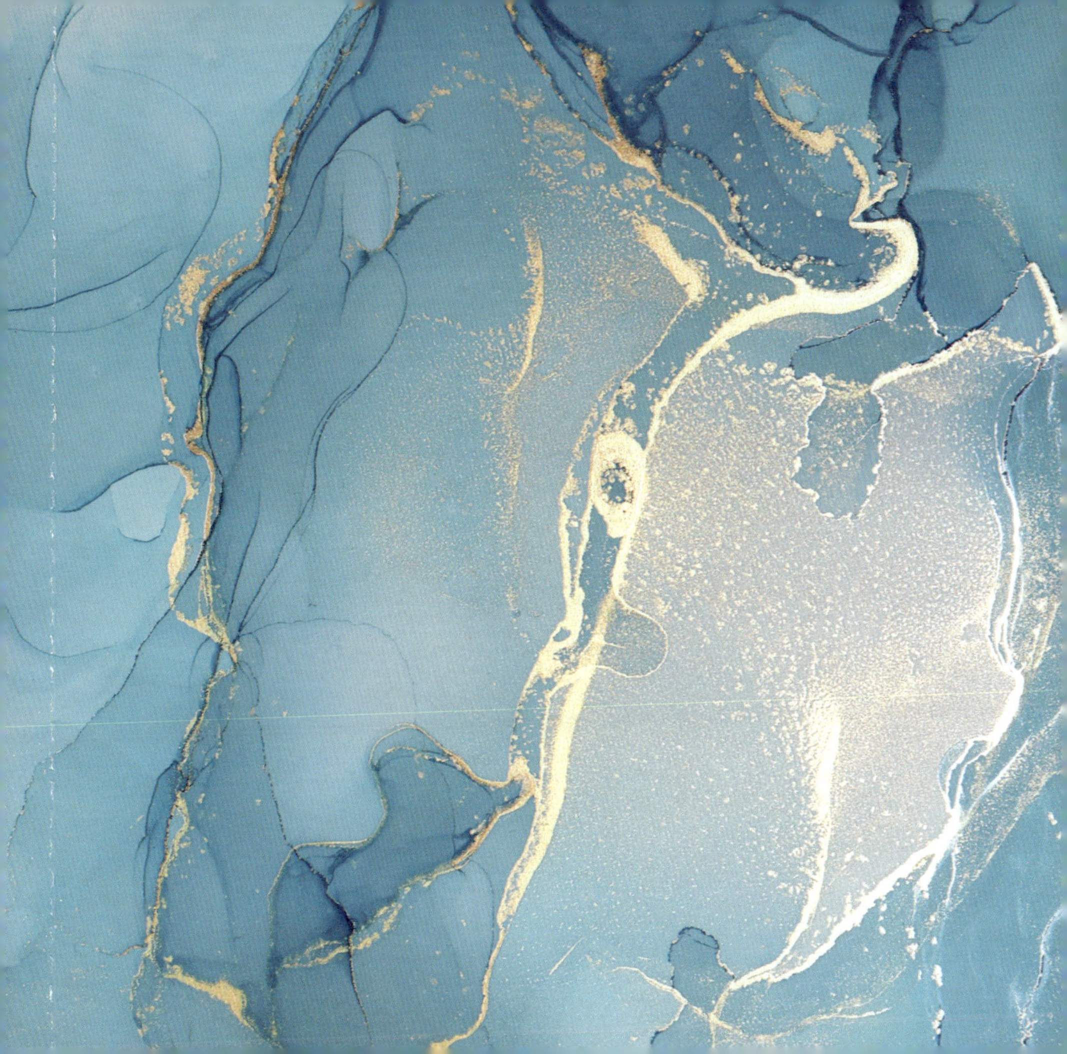

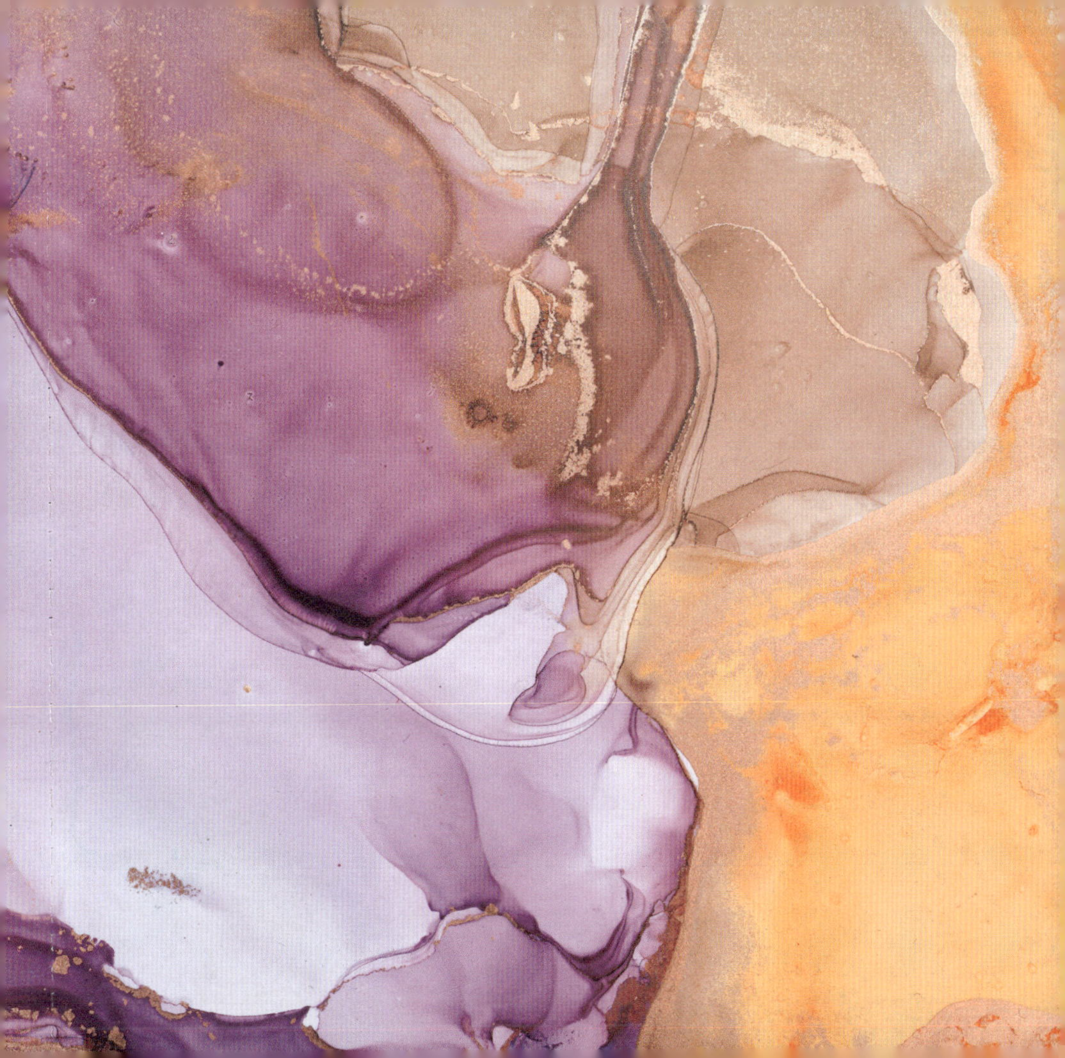

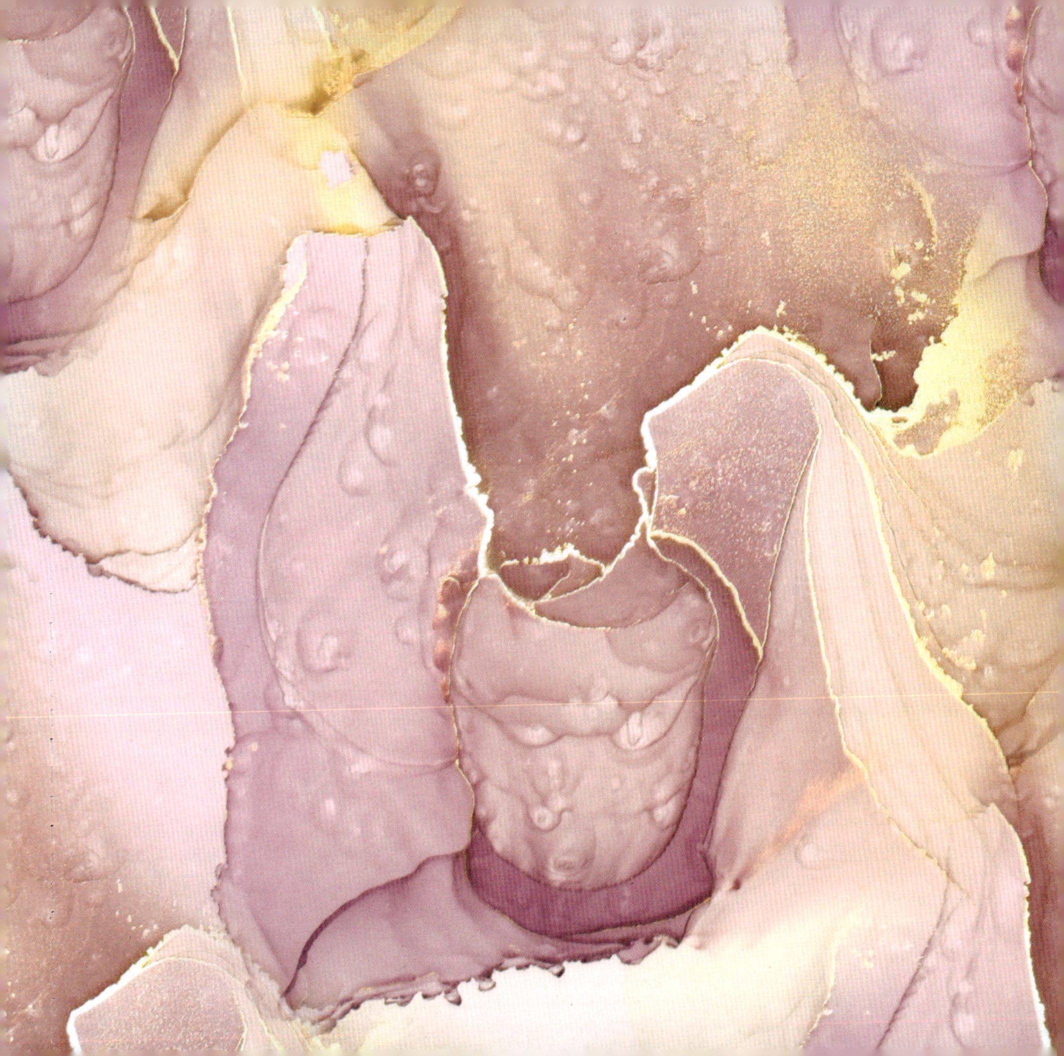

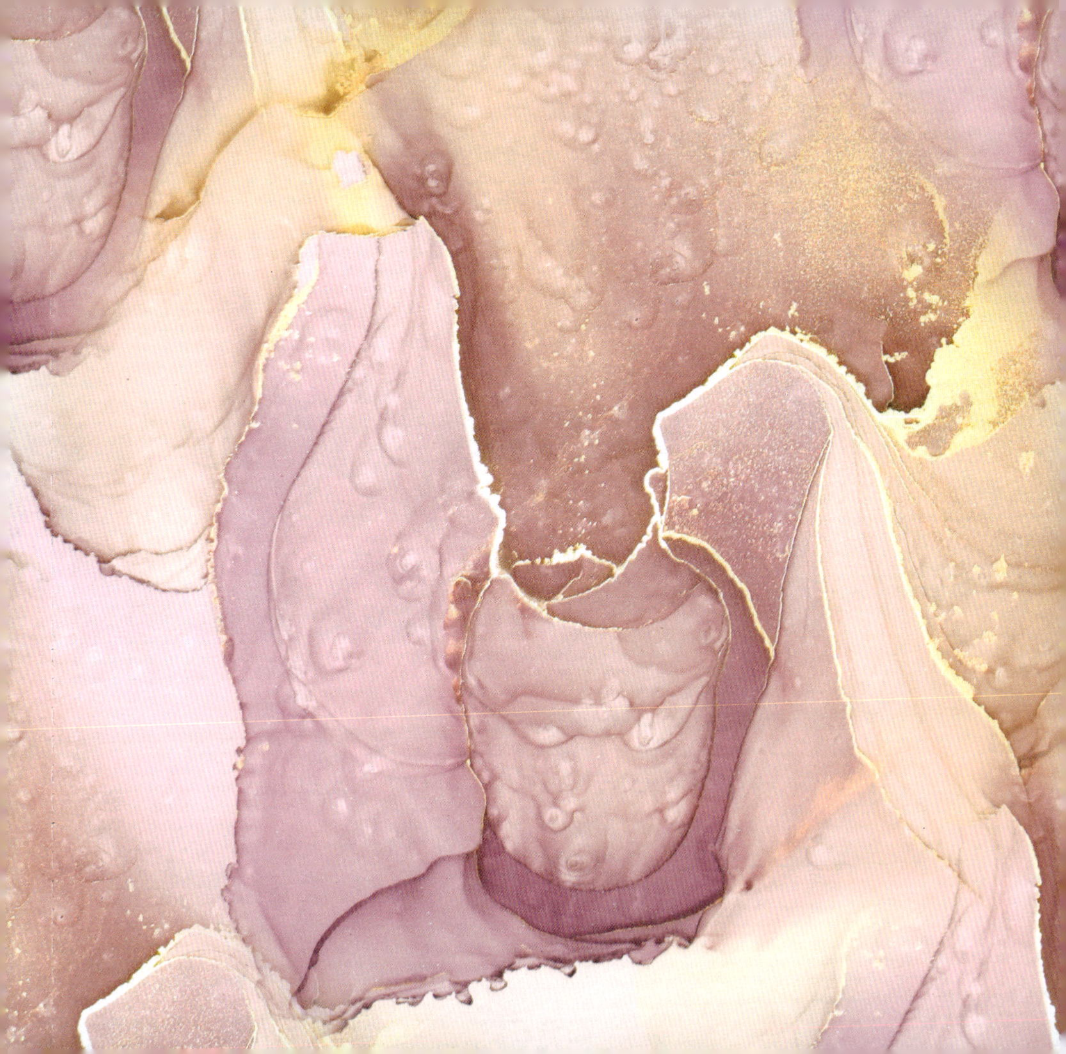

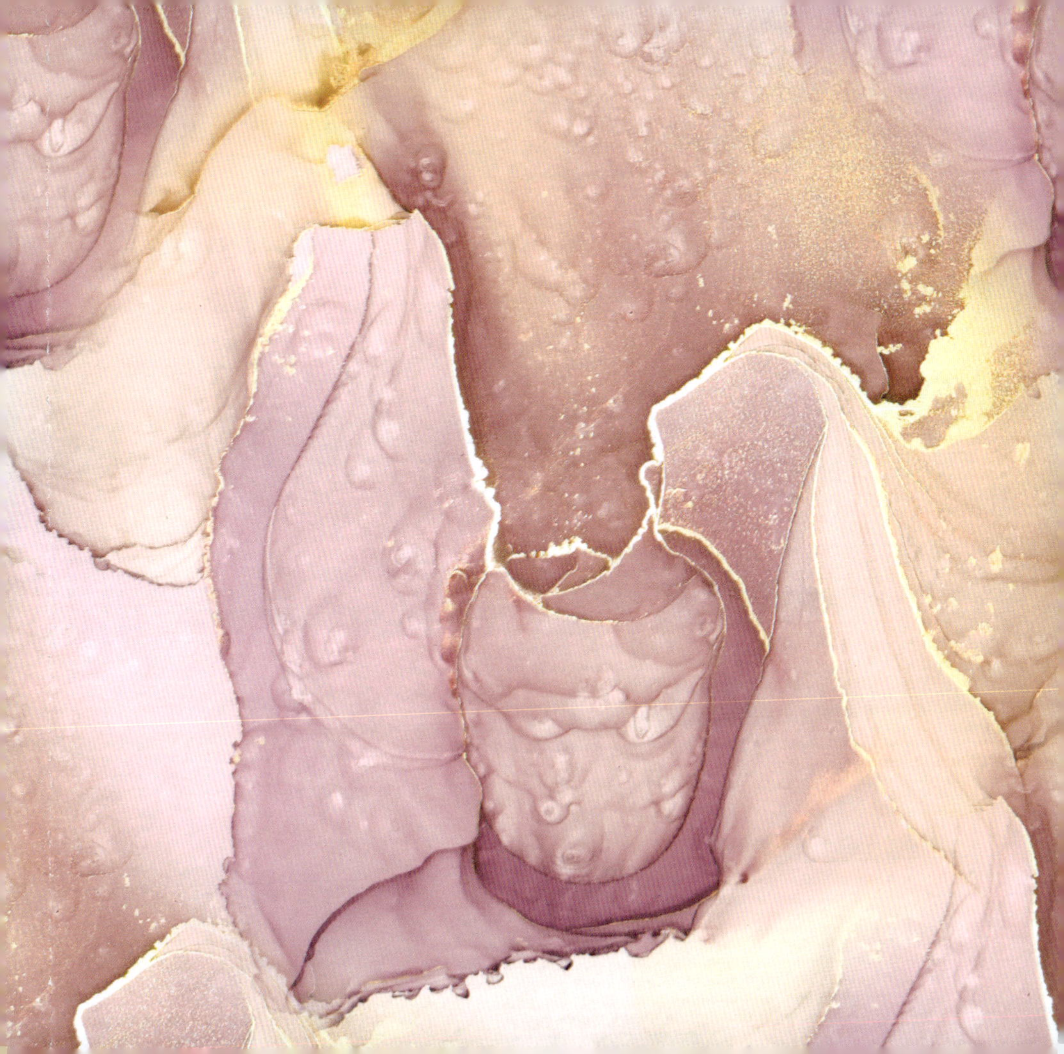

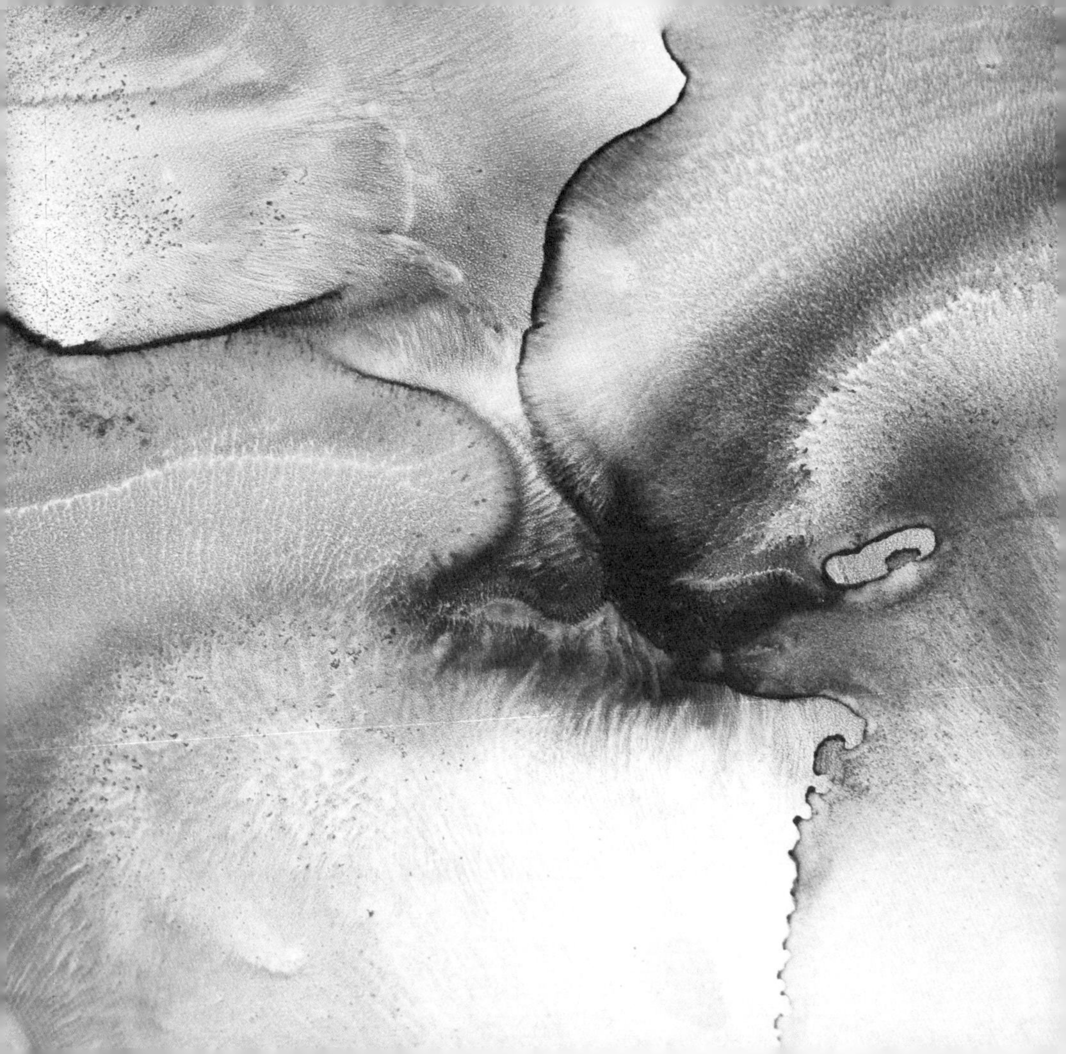

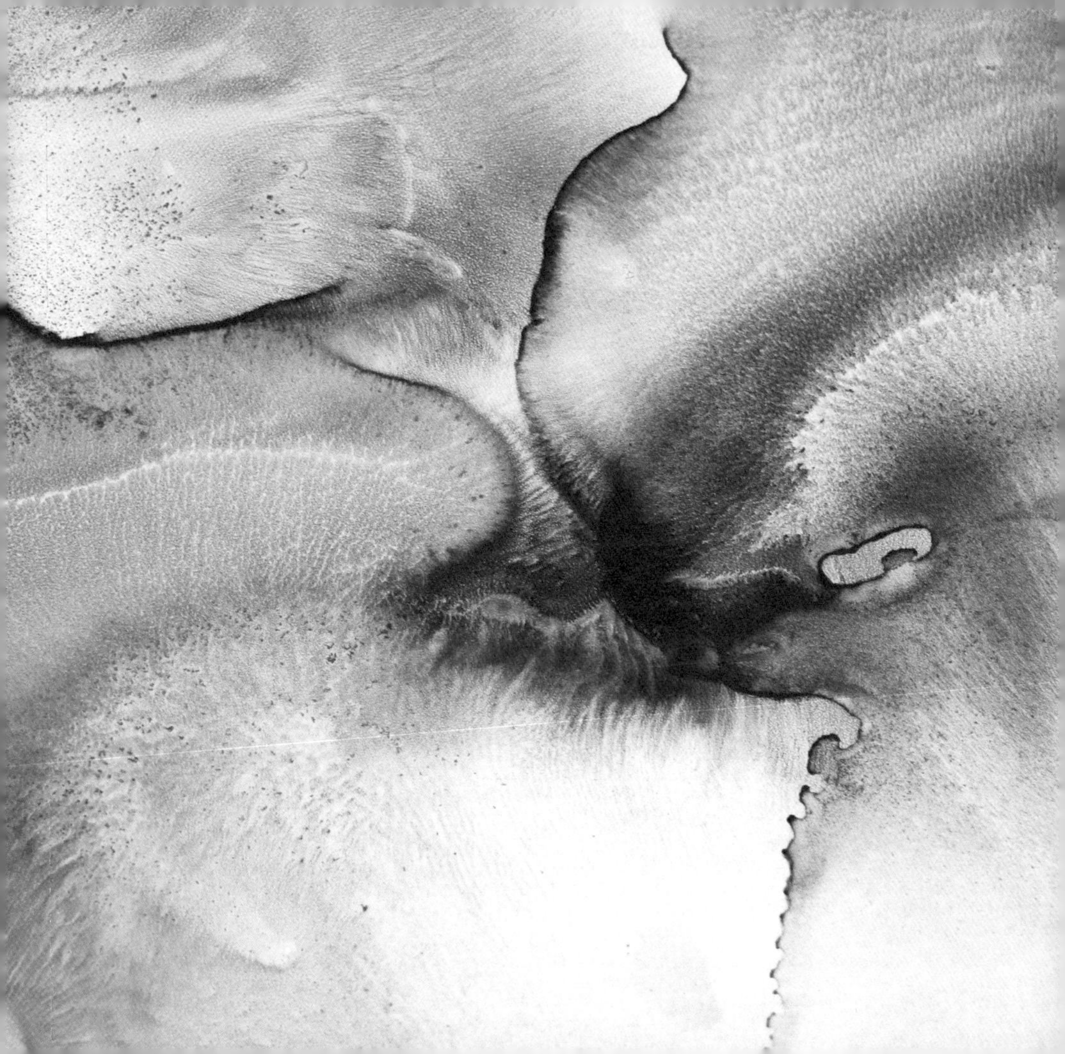

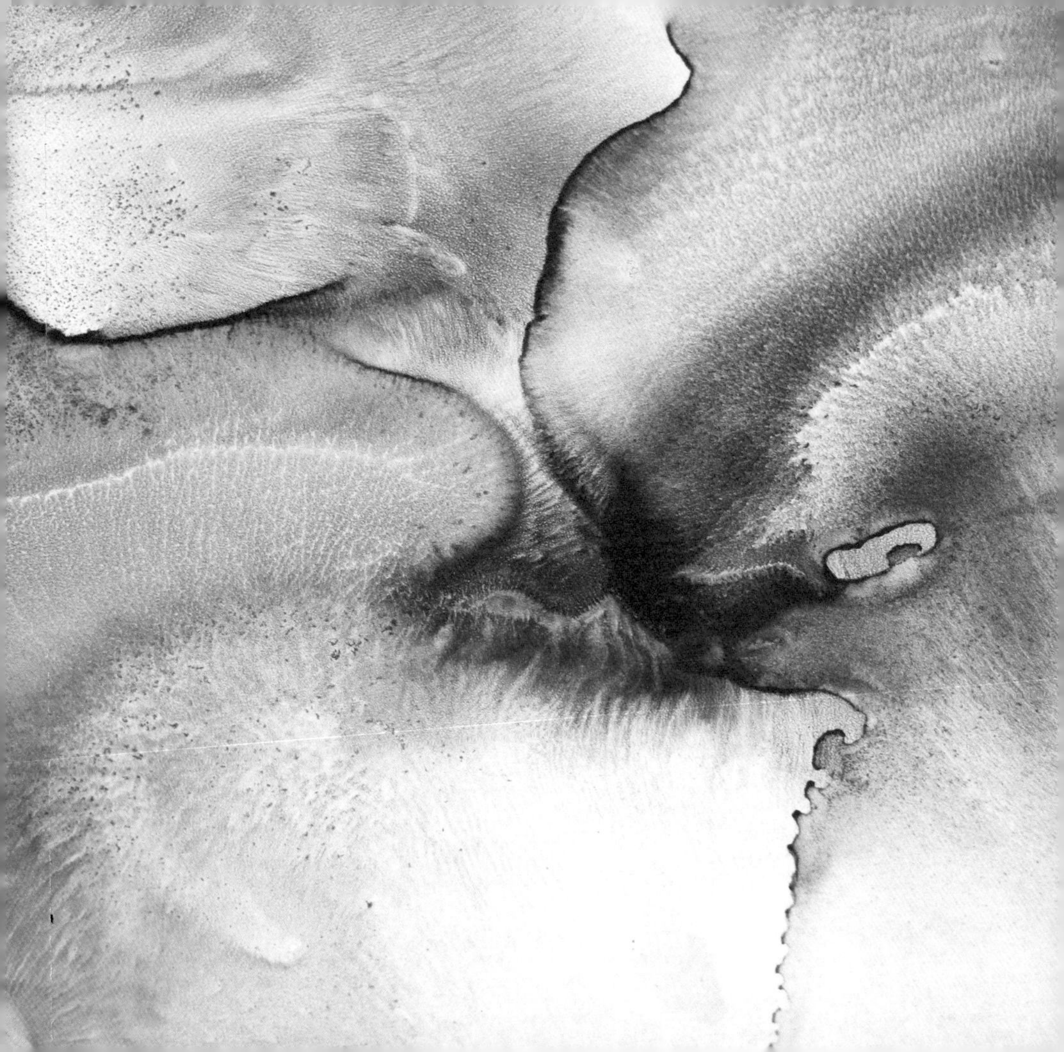

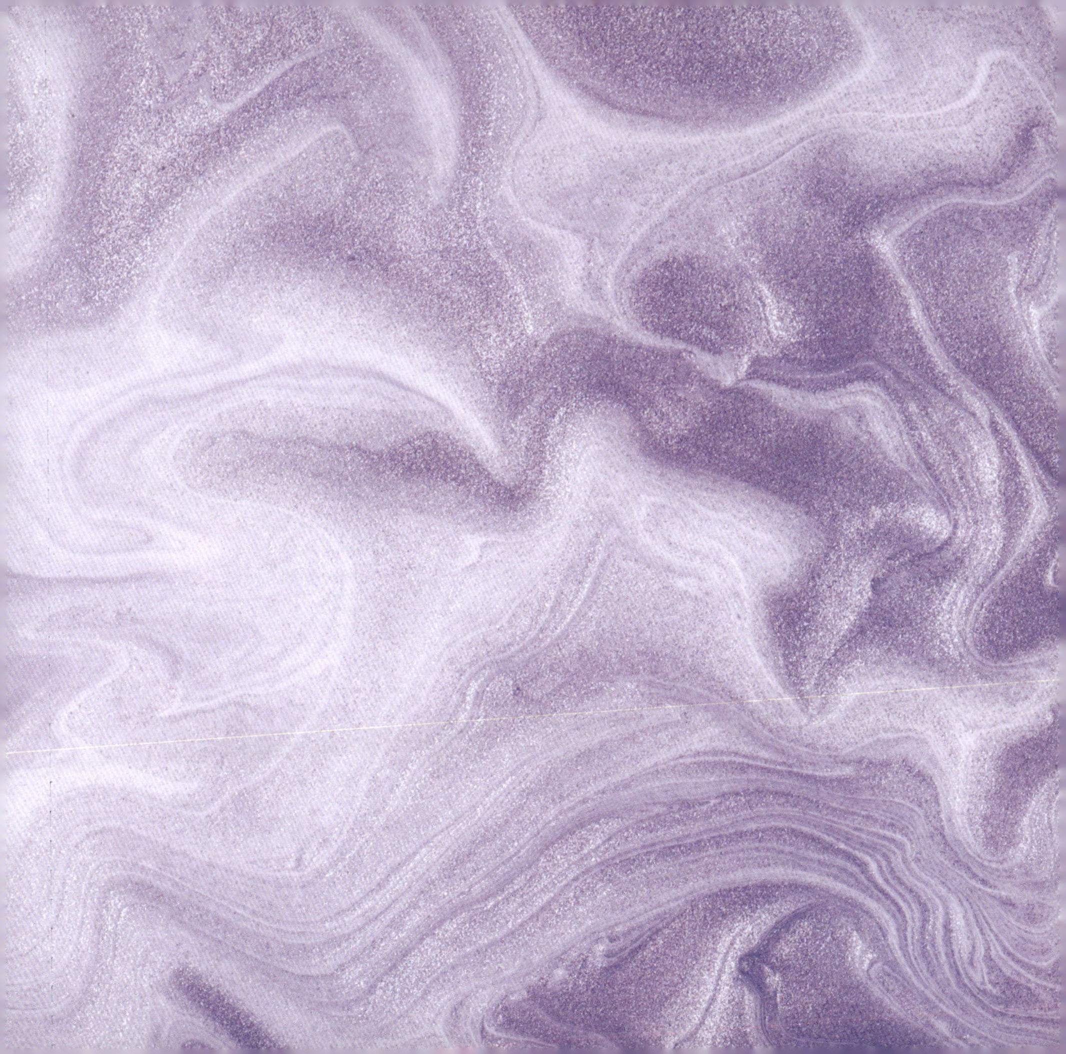

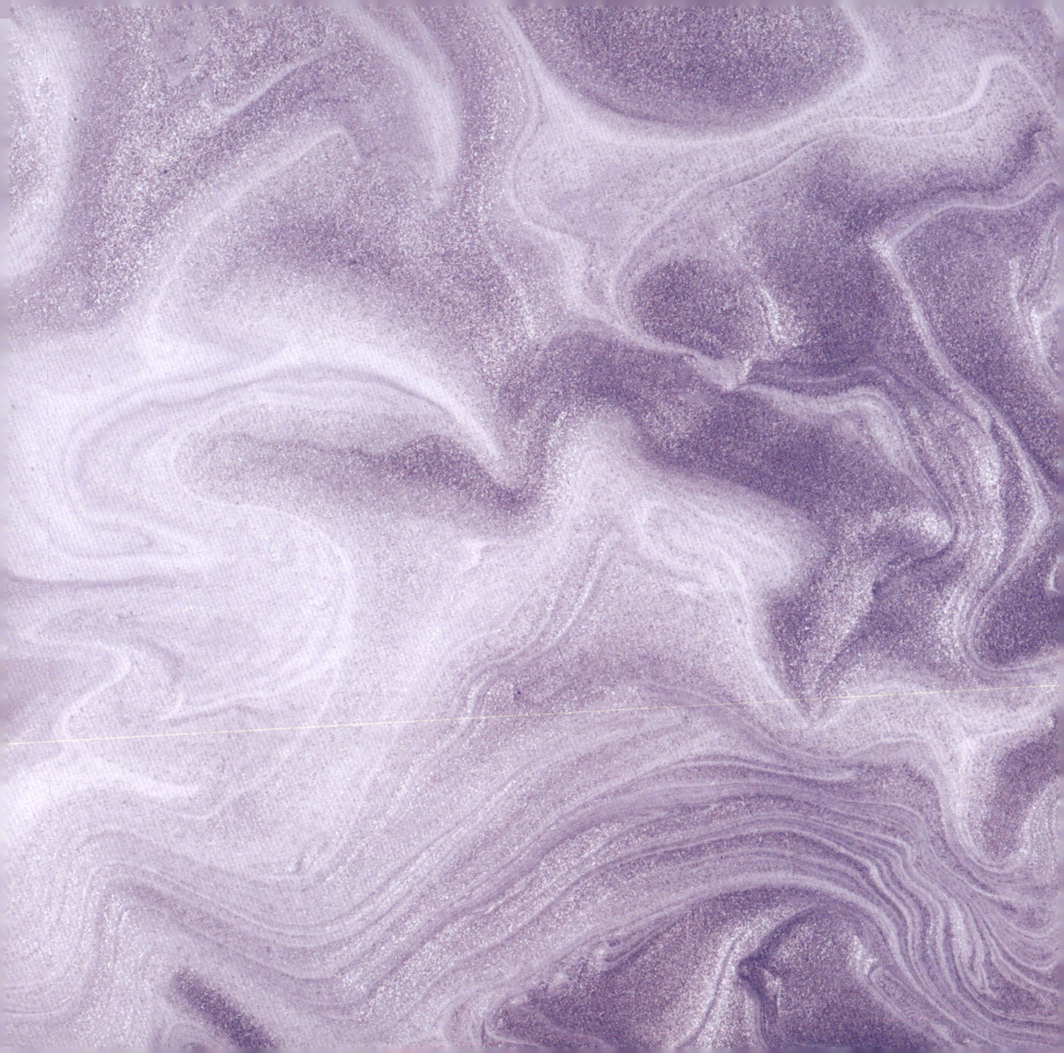

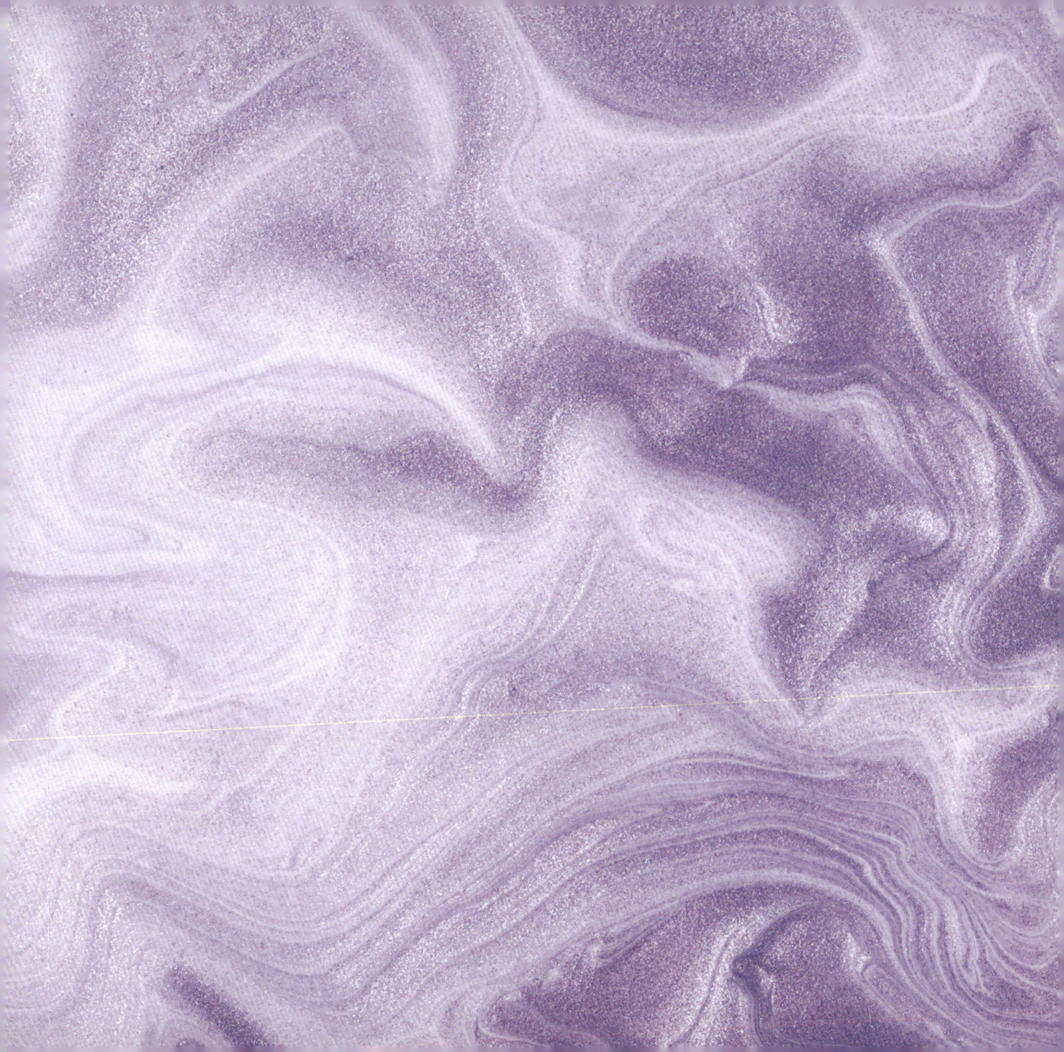

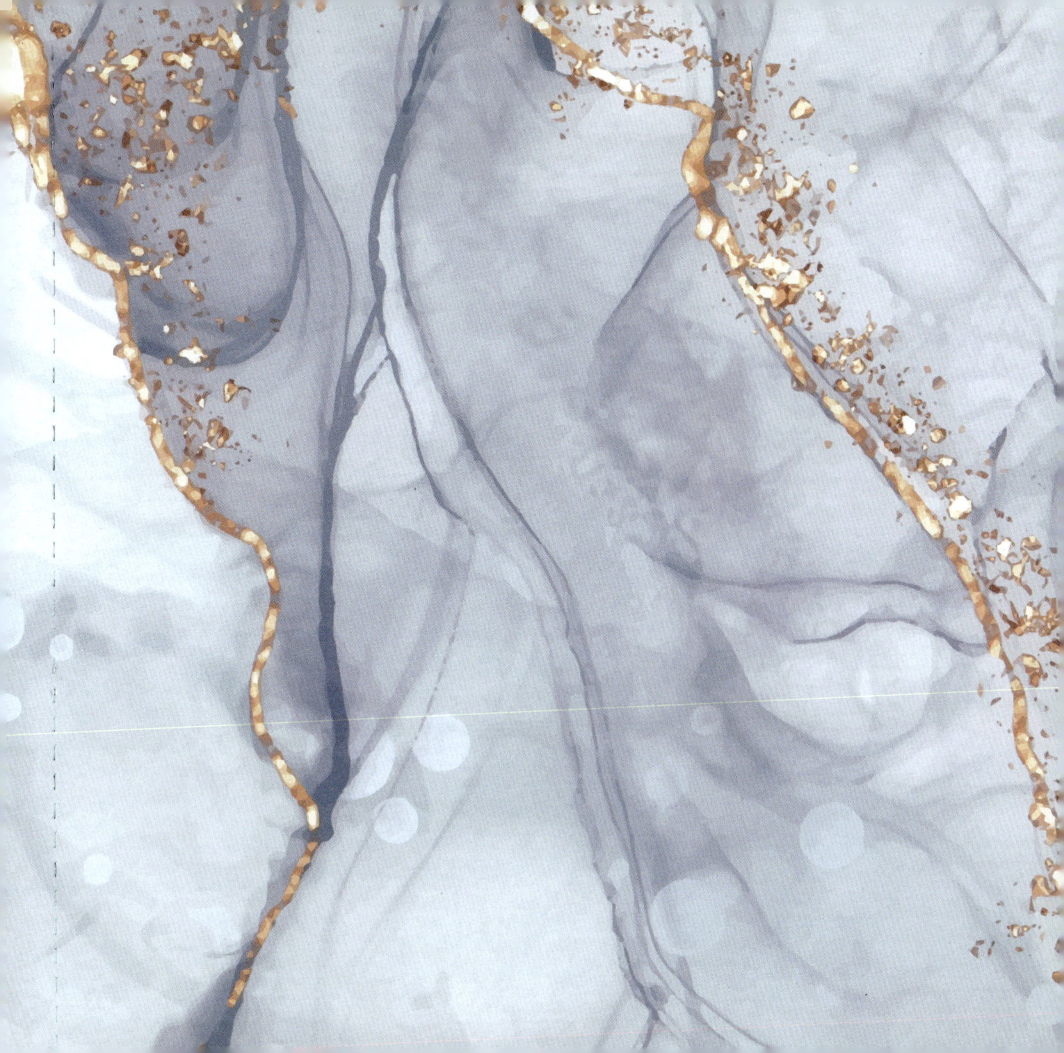

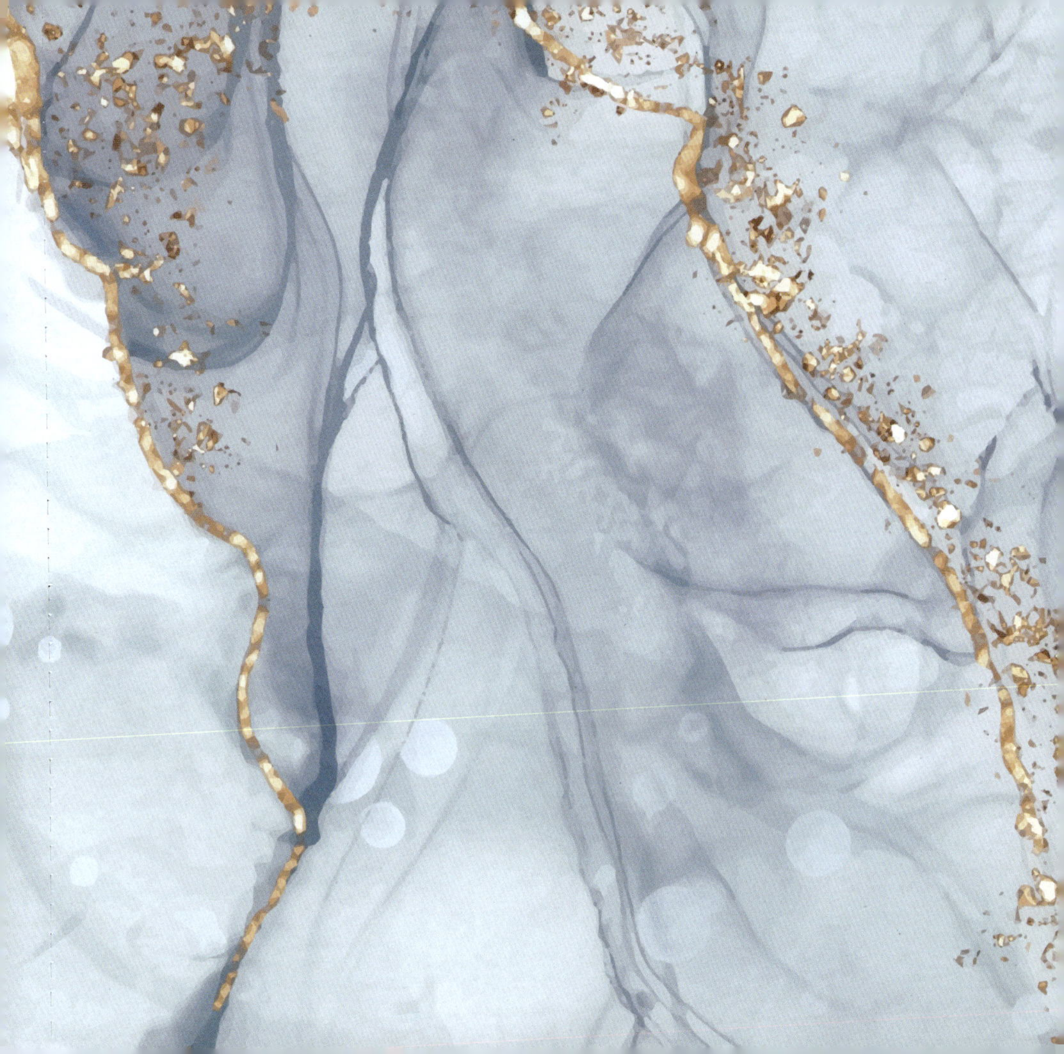

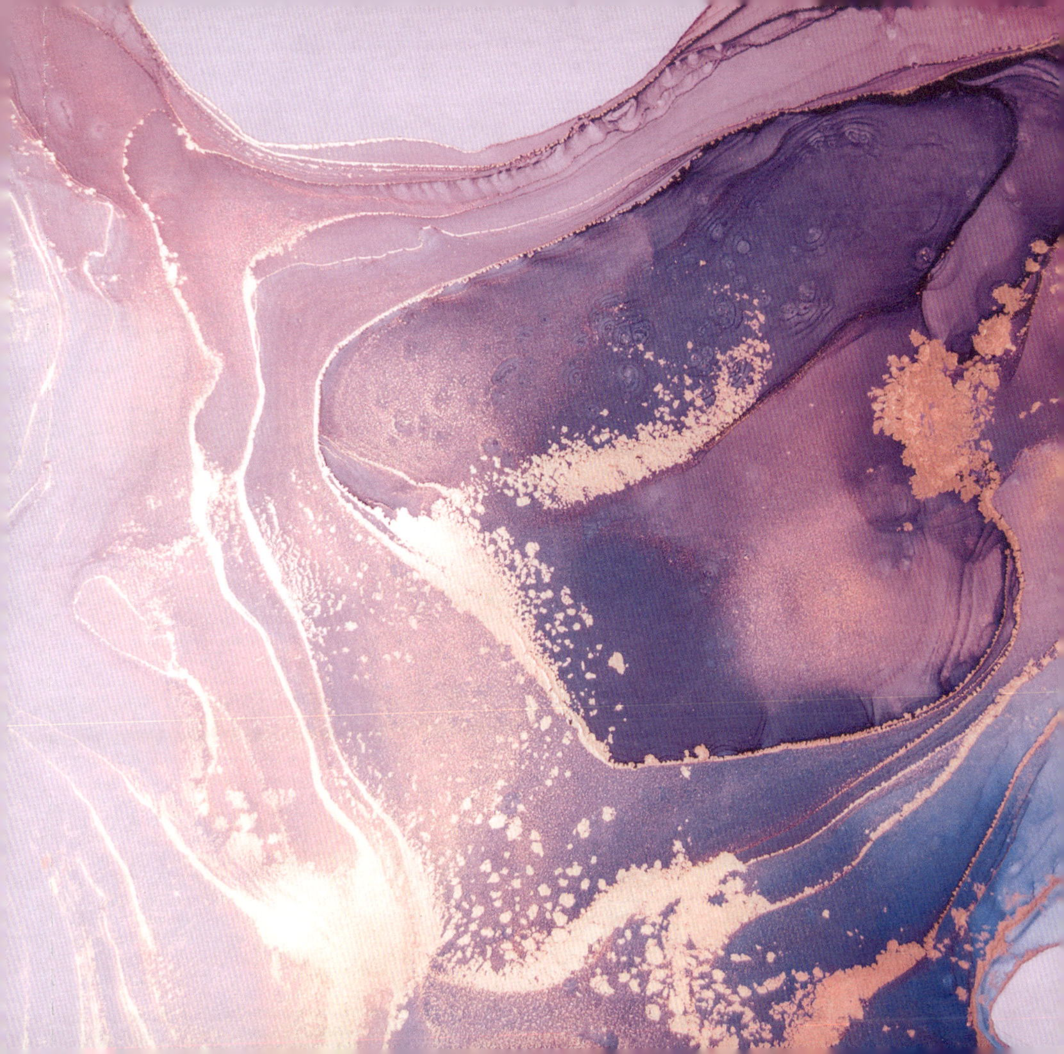

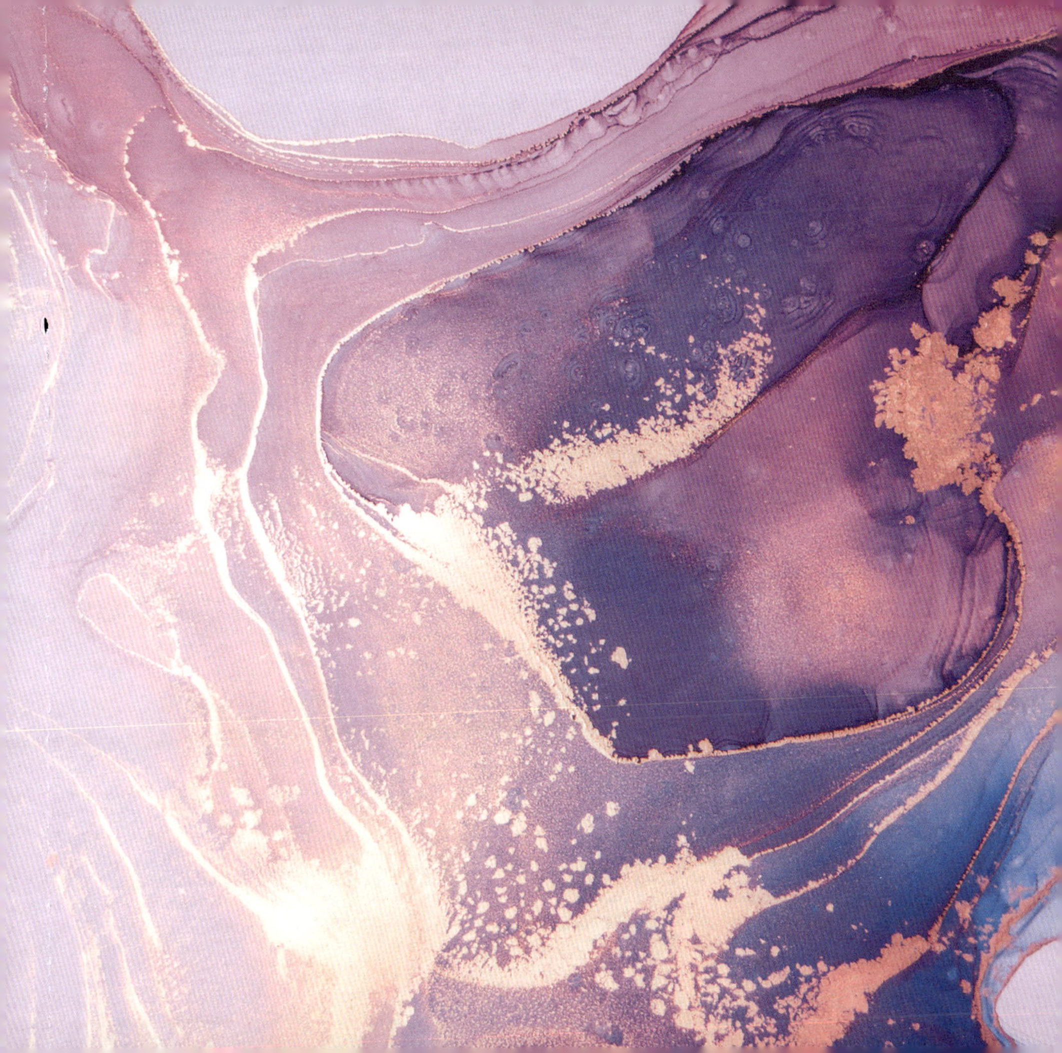

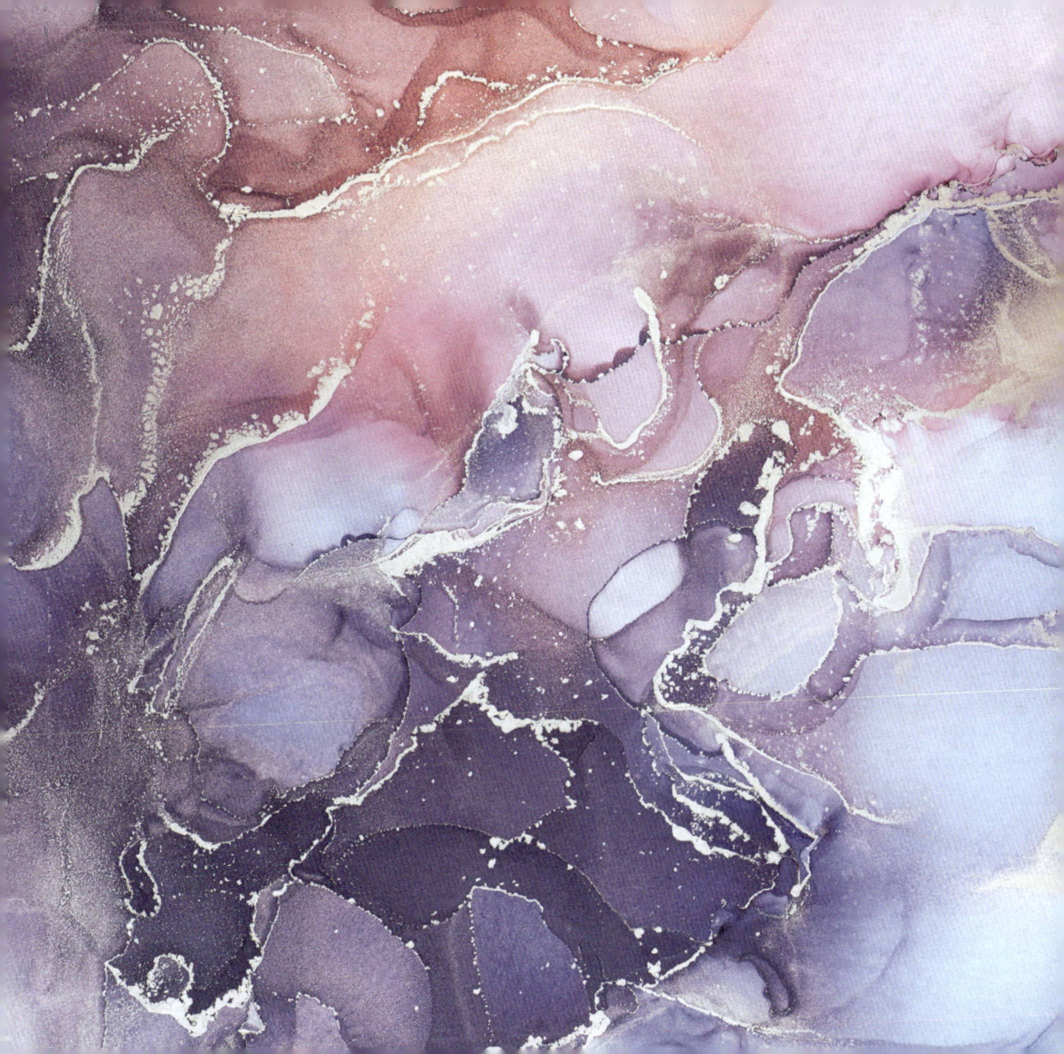

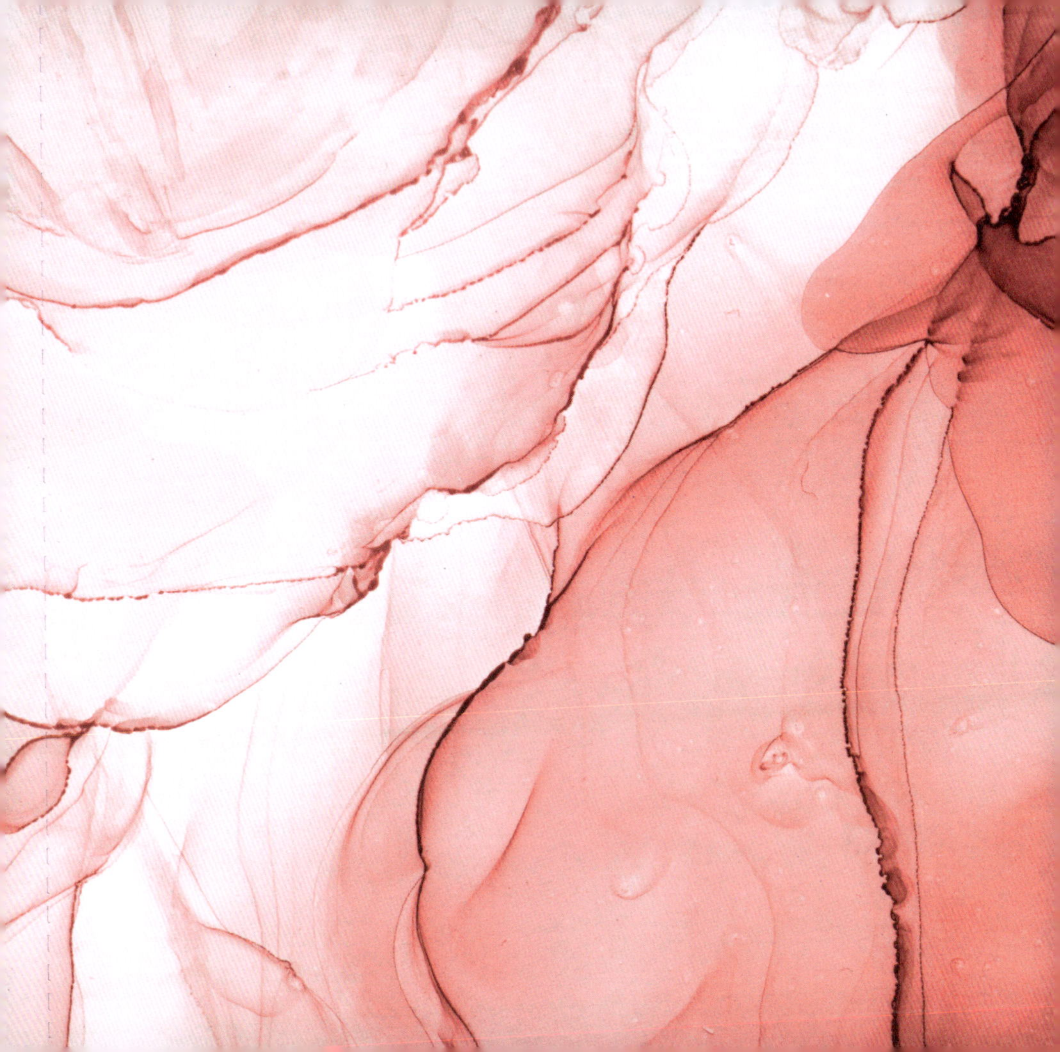

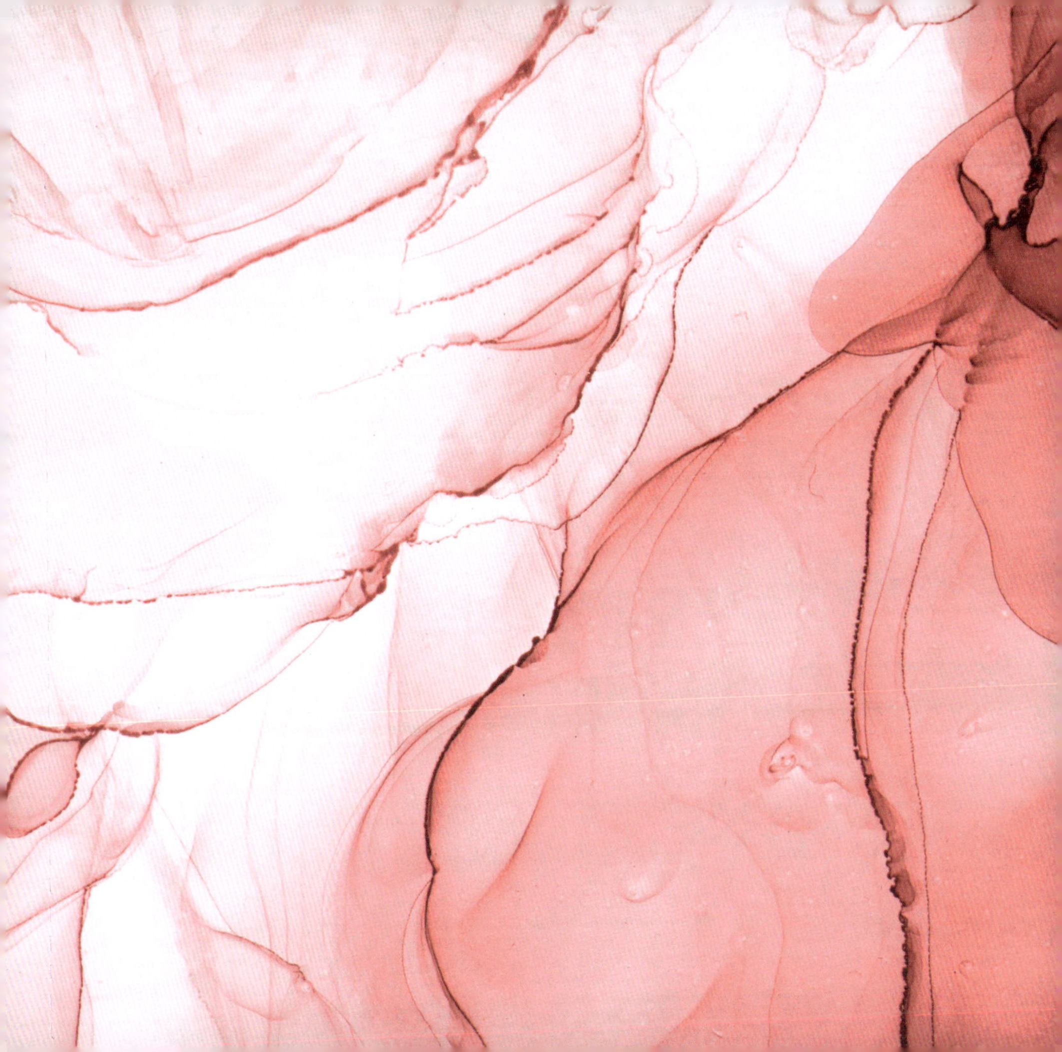

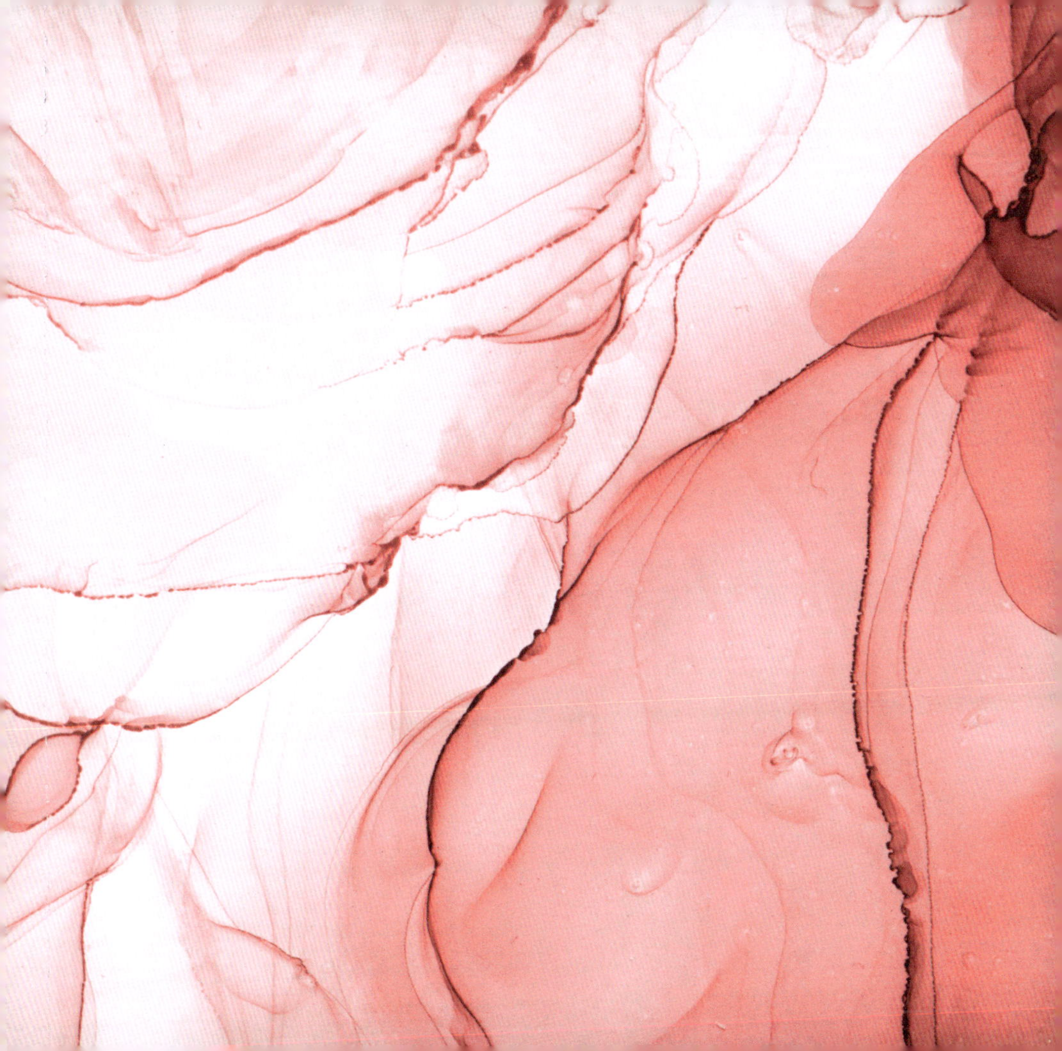

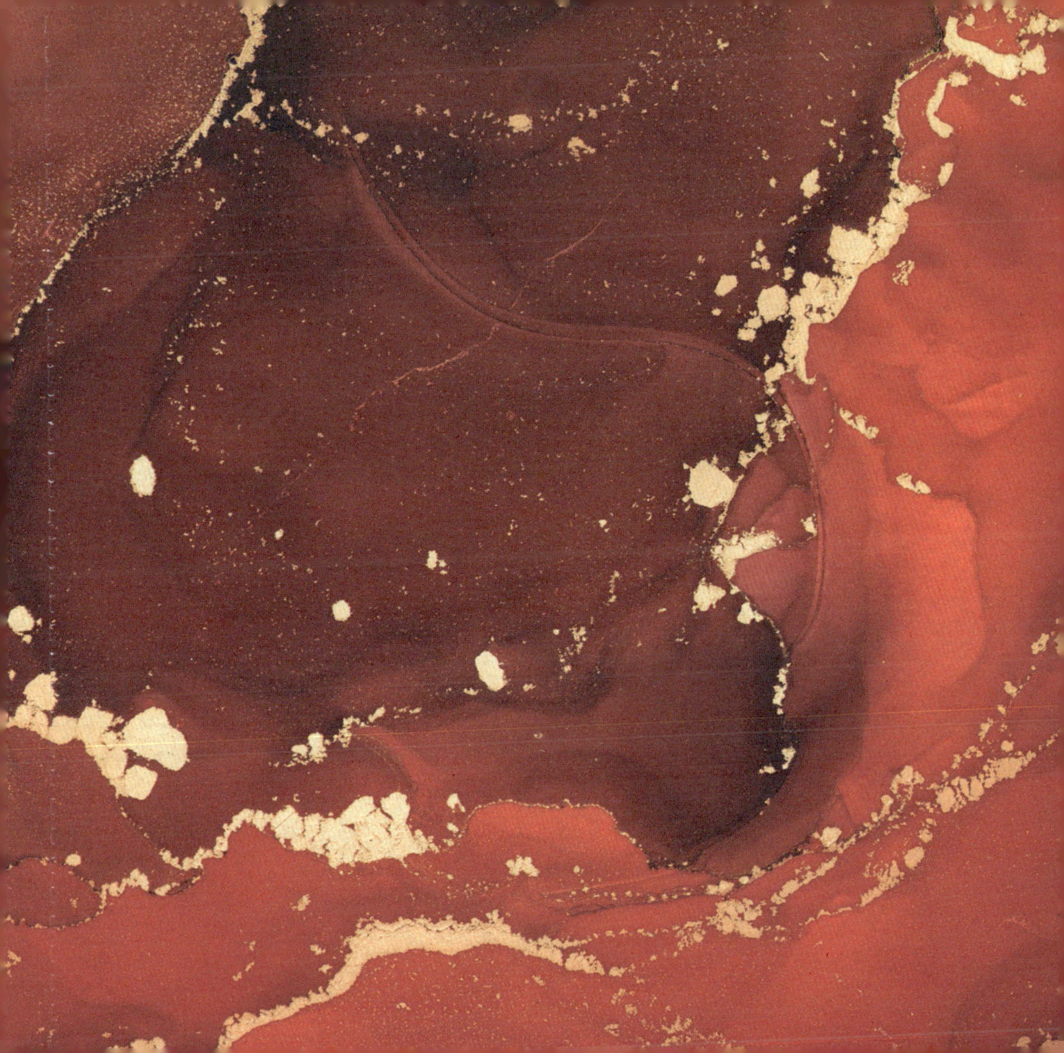

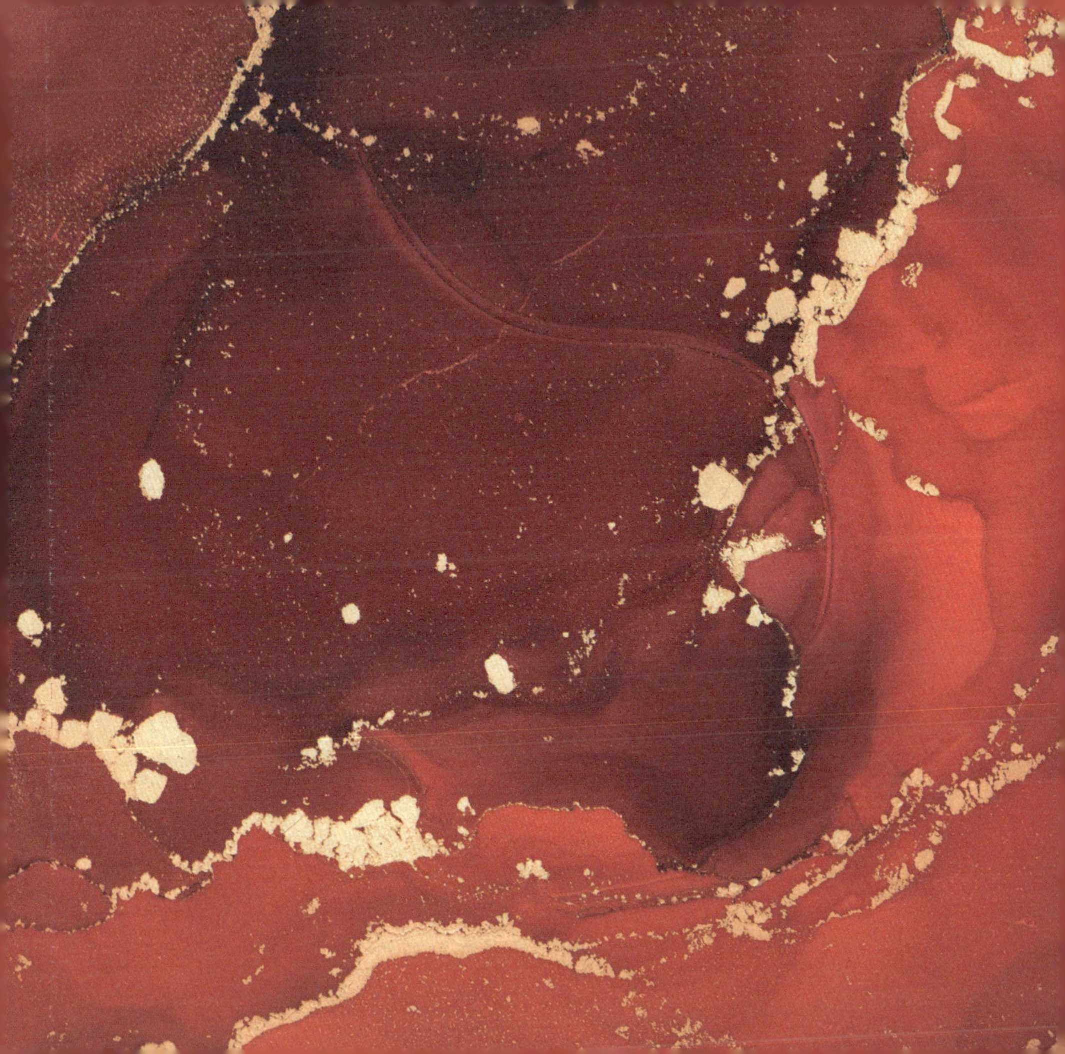